Brave New Girl

End people pleasing, discover the power
of 'no' and become your
most confident self

Chloe Brotheridge, BSc, DipH, DipNLP, HC, is a clinical hypnotherapist and certified coach who specializes in helping people who suffer from anxiety and confidence issues. Chloe has her own practice in London and has helped hundreds of sufferers overcome severe anxiety.

Having suffered from anxiety, low self-esteem and confidence issues since her teens, and having found her own path to inner healing, Chloe now feels privileged to be able to share with others the transformative tools and techniques she used herself to achieve a sense of self-worth, courage and confidence.

@ChloeBrotheridge

Brave New Girl

End people pleasing,
discover the power of 'no'
and become your most
confident self

CHLOE BROTHERIDGE

MICHAEL JOSEPH
an imprint of
PENGUIN BOOKS

MICHAEL JOSEPH

UK | USA | Canada | Ireland | Australia
India | New Zealand | South Africa

Michael Joseph is part of the Penguin Random House group of companies
whose addresses can be found at global.penguinrandomhouse.com

First published 2019

001

Copyright © Chloe Brotheridge, 2019

The moral right of the author has been asserted

Part title illustrations: Agne Alesiute
p. 287, The Feelings Wheel taken from 'The Feeling Wheel' by Gloria Willcox
in *The Transactional Analysis Journal*, vol. 12, issue 4, (Taylor & Francis, 1 Oct 1982),
reprinted by permission of the publisher.

Every effort has been made to trace copyright holders and to obtain
their permission for the use of copyright material. The publisher apologizes for any
errors or omissions and would be grateful to be notified of any corrections
that should be incorporated in future editions of this book.

Set in Garamond MT and Gotham
Typeset by Penguin Books

Printed in Great Britain by Clays Ltd, Elcograf S.p.A.

A CIP catalogue record for this book is available from the British Library

ISBN: 978–0–241–40043–2

www.greenpenguin.co.uk

MIX
Paper from
responsible sources
FSC
www.fsc.org FSC® C018179

Penguin Random House is committed to a
sustainable future for our business, our readers
and our planet. This book is made from Forest
Stewardship Council® certified paper.

To the brave women reading this book.

Contents

PART THREE
How to stop apologizing for
yourself – and say NO

PART FOUR
How to fail yourself better

PART FIVE
How to heal shame and self-doubt

Contents

Acknowledgements

Thank you so much to my agent Valeria Huerta for always believing in me and encouraging me. I feel very blessed that we met and that I get to work with you.

Thank you to Fenella Bates at Penguin for trusting in my idea for this book and for all your kindness and positive energy. Huge thanks to everyone at Penguin for all their hard work on the book.

I am very grateful to Brigid Moss for editing the book, for her wisdom and patience and for working in between Christmas and New Year so that we could get it finished in time! I felt the book was in very safe hands with you.

Thank you so much to my mum and dad for being so loving, supportive and fun. For all your encouragement, acceptance and unconditional love. And for my sweetheart sisters Olivia and Charlotte for being so loving. Thanks in advance to my granny, also known as my PR woman, who I know will be encouraging everyone in her village to buy this book. And thank you, Granny, for giving me the best gift ever, Transcendental Meditation.

Thanks to Emily and Vicky for being there to help me sound out ideas and for being the first readers of the book. And to Bonnie and Bonnie for all the supportive chats!

I'm so grateful for Aidan, for being rock solid in his love and support, a constant source of inspiration and for putting up with me when I ignored him because I was writing this book. I'm a much braver person because you are in my life!

Thank you to the reader, it feels like a massive privilege to write a book – thank you for supporting me. You are brave, you are strong, and you've got this!

Introduction

How would you act, if you didn't care what people thought?

Who would you be, if you knew for sure you were worthy, loved and accepted?

What would you do, if you knew failure was just a stepping stone, not a final resting place?

How much more time and energy would you have, if you could confidently say no and ask for what you want?

Chances are, if you're picking up this book, you've been playing a much smaller game than you're capable of. For a long time, you've had a hunch there's another way of living that, until now, has been beyond your grasp. You know, if only you could let go of the burden of worrying what people think, you'd do things very differently. You sense it's time to take up a bit more space, to speak a little louder, to be OK with being seen. It's time to cast off the layers of fear, insecurity and negative beliefs about yourself that have weighed you down. And to reveal the real you, who is capable, strong, confident and worthy.

Women tell me time and time again about their constant worries about other people's opinions, about the pressure to look perfect and the crippling self-doubt and shyness that keeps them from speaking up. About the strain of needing to say yes to every request and invite, which leaves them burnt out and overwhelmed. And about the angst of trying to please everyone, all of the time.

I too have felt broken, unworthy and ashamed, just for being myself.

I've gone to extraordinary lengths to avoid situations where I might get criticized because it just felt too painful.

I've been mute and red-faced in meetings because I felt my ideas weren't worth sharing.

I have shaken with fear because I felt like a fraud about to be found out at any moment.

I didn't dare to dream because I thought I'd never amount to anything.

I've found it impossible to ask for what I want (even from my boyfriend) because I was scared of the other person's reaction.

I've censored myself, dumbed myself down and agreed to things I didn't believe in because I wanted people to like me.

But I'm not doing any of that any more. And my hope is, after reading this book, you won't have to, either. This book is all about becoming the most confident version of yourself: bold, strong and self-assured. It's about owning your own inner bravery and using that to move past your comfort zone and towards fulfilling your beautiful potential.

After all, we're living in a new world with infinite opportunities . . . if only we could get past the things holding us back. Most of us would like more confidence – but why is it so elusive? It seems like some women are just born with it, with a boldness that's second nature. And it's true; some people do find it easier to be more confident than others.

But what if you're not one of those natural-born assertive types? What if you're a people pleaser and crippled with self-doubt? What if saying no to your partner already seems too much, let alone asking your manager for a pay rise? For those of us who don't currently have iron-clad confidence, there's good news. And it is this: confidence isn't a trait that you're either blessed with or not. In fact, it's a skill you can develop, learn and improve on. It's a state of mind you can cultivate. And it's an action that you can start taking right now.

How to use this book

This book will lead you through the inner journey of learning to care less about what others think, healing the shame and fear of failure that's kept you stuck in shyness, people pleasing and playing small. Next, we'll move on to the practical steps you can take to grow your confidence, ask for what you want (and get it), help you find your voice and live the free life of limitless potential you've always wanted.

My suggestion would be to read this book as if you're doing a course step by step. I highly recommend taking some notes as you go, to remind yourself of the insights most relevant to you, and keeping a journal handy to make note of the exercises that speak to you most. Alternatively, you could also skim through and choose the sections that are most relevant to you, coming back to the other sections at a later stage.

Make sure you download the free bonuses that accompany this book at www.calmer-you.com/brave-bonus where you'll find worksheets and meditation MP3s to support your courage and confidence as you read this book.

PART ONE

How to start the change

CHAPTER 1

Why I wrote this book
for women

Despite tremendous strides in reaching equality with men, we all know there's still a way to go. We grew up seeing our mothers and grandmothers doing the majority of the child-rearing, cooking and cleaning. We were raised to be caregivers and nurturers, and given dolls and Sylvanian Families to play with (although we may have been given Lego, too).

Society has different expectations for little girls and little boys. I'm generalizing here, but we're more likely to be molly-coddled and warned to stay safe. By the way, I by no means want to take away from the struggles that men experience, but the female experience has particular qualities. Many of us have been conditioned into believing the importance of keeping others happy and appearing 'perfect'; a 2016 study by Girl Guiding found that a quarter of girls said they felt under pressure to be perfect. A third said people made them feel as though the way they look is the most important thing about them.[1] Women are twice as likely to suffer from anxiety as men, according to The Mental Health Foundation.[2]

We're taught not to brag, to be modest at all times. How many of us heard 'don't be a show-off' when we were younger? Who still finds it hard to accept a compliment, for fear you'll appear big-headed?

Our conditioning goes back generations; parents pass on their fears, doubts and limiting beliefs to their children. And it was only a hundred years – three generations – ago that women got the vote. When my great-grandmother was born, women were still expected to forgo an education or a career. Even if they worked, the focus was on the domestic sphere and raising children.

In the majority of households it's still women who take time off work to raise children (and later, to look after elderly parents) – although more men are doing so. And while times are changing, beliefs in society still hang around in our collective subconscious, however equally your parents tried to raise you, or you are trying to raise your children. They include doubts and expectations such as:

- Women shouldn't get angry. They should be agreeable, polite and play nice.
- If a woman is confident, she's bossy or arrogant.
- Cleaning is women's work. A government analysis showed women do 60 per cent more unpaid work (for example, housework, cooking and childcare) than their male partners.[3]
- Women should be the primary carers for children and elderly relatives.
- Women should keep other people happy and put everyone before themselves.
- Women should look good at all times, spend years of their lives, thousands of pounds and stacks of energy on their appearance.
- Women who take care of themselves or say no are selfish.
- Women should be as thin as possible and not take up too much space.
- If a woman is sexually demanding, she's a slut.
- When a woman stands up for herself, she's a bitch.

You've probably never considered that your confidence might be higher if you were male. But it seems likely. For example, men tend to overestimate their IQ, but women are more likely to underestimate theirs.[4] And a man will apply for a job if he feels he meets 60 per cent of the requirements, while a woman will only do so when she's sure she meets 100 per cent, according to a study by Hewlett Packard.[5]

What I've experienced, both in myself and in my clients, is we don't trust our own opinions and we fear failure or criticism, so we play safe or we don't try at all. We're scared to speak up in case we say the 'wrong' thing or hurt people's feelings. We're less likely to take risks, we're more prone to taking criticism to heart. Across our lives women have, on average, consistently lower self-esteem than men.[6] All of this can mean our confidence – along with our career prospects – takes a knock.

After babies, it's more often the woman who returns part-time or to a smaller job, often meaning her career ambitions need to be scaled down, too. Sadly, good girls finish last. At work, not being confident of your value could mean you don't negotiate, charge or value your worth. And women who don't go back to work after children risk losing our identity, building up resentment or ending up burning out because our own needs don't get met.

There's no denying cultural norms, and the structure of society can be crushing to a woman's confidence. But on an individual level, you can decide to break free. And as each of us starts to change, we will be changing things at a collective level, too.

Falling into the beauty trap

As a small girl, I dreamed of having a Disney princess dress. At the age of eleven, I saved for weeks to buy an overpriced hair serum to solve my frizzy hair 'problem' (it didn't) after reading about it in a magazine. I was moisturizing from the age of nine and skipping meals in order to try to achieve a flat stomach at fourteen. All I wanted was a skinny frame like Marissa from *The O.C.* In my early twenties I was certain the only way a boy would ever look at me was if I had the swishy, tumbling curls and killer abs of a Victoria's Secret model.

Have you ever wanted to look different from the way you look in the mirror – maybe straighter hair, smaller thighs, smaller nose? I did, constantly. Looking back, it's as if I swallowed whole every ideal of female attractiveness that I came across. At first glance, this focus on looks may seem superficial but the truth is, how we feel about our bodies and appearance has enormous consequences for our ability to be assertive and confident in all areas of our life. Body-image concerns impact mental health in the all-important teen years. According to the Dove Global Beauty and Confidence Report, only 20 per cent of UK women like their appearance, the lowest body confidence level in the world. Having poor body confidence impacts whether girls will be assertive in their opinions and stick to their decisions.[7]

As a woman, *thinking* that you are 'fat' has a pronounced impact on depressive symptoms (regardless of your actual weight).[8] Women worry about looks more than men (that's not to say men don't have their own body issues too). Men tend to think they're thinner than their actual weight, whereas women tend to think they're heavier.[9]

Body image feeds into self-esteem, which in turn affects academic achievement and earning power. Eating and body-image issues have been found to have a negative impact on academic achievement.[10] Lower body-esteem can impact how attractive you feel, and so affect both the quality of your sex life and your long-term relationships.[11]

The truth is, at every age and stage, we have been confronted with a perfect ideal that is impossible to reach. In my training as a hypnotherapist, I learned that as we zone out in front of the TV, we enter a trance state where we're more open to the suggestions and messages we see and hear on the screen. It's a form of hypnosis; advertisers capitalize on this to convince you their products are the answer to all your problems. Suddenly, eating crappy breakfast cereal for every meal in order to starve yourself into smaller jeans, and believing your 'frizz' desperately needs to be eased by overpriced goop, seems totally reasonable!

We are what we eat – and much of the media feed we consume is junk. We've grown up on a diet of *Gossip Girl*, *Britain's Next Top Model* and *Beach Body SOS* and it has poisoned our confidence. Your thighs are not the problem, the culture is. The Dove report also found that over half of girls in the UK have avoided doing an activity such as going for dinner, joining a debate or playing sports because of concerns about how they look.

How much more amazing and powerful would we be as women if body-image issues didn't handicap us?

Living in this society, with its unrealistic expectations and pressures, it's up to you to act courageously and recapture your confidence.

How your childhood impacts your confidence

Your life is shaped by your beliefs. A belief is simply a thought you have accepted to be true. We have all taken on board beliefs through different experiences, among them the cultural norms we've just been discussing. But the most toxic beliefs that hold us back have their roots in life events we often don't talk about enough: trauma.

Dig down from anxiety, depression and self-confidence issues and you'll often find trauma at the root. Please don't be put off by the 't' word. You don't have to have experienced huge negative events to suffer the effects of trauma. In fact, there are two types of trauma, big 'T' trauma and little 't' trauma. Big 'T' includes what you'd normally call trauma: serious events such as being caught up in natural disasters, wars, terrorist incidents, accidents and being a victim of sexual assault or any crime.

One big 'T' trauma that's sadly very common and can have a big impact on confidence in later life is sexual assault. Childhood sexual abuse is a real problem; 11 per cent of women have suffered this, according to the Office for National Statistics, and it can have far-reaching consequences later in life.[12] The Crime Survey for England and Wales (CSEW) revealed that a shocking 1 in 5 women and 1 in 25 men have experienced some type of sexual assault as adults.[13] And it's estimated 3.1 per cent of women have experienced a sexual assault in the last year alone.[14]

Then there are little 't's. These are experiences that many, in fact probably most, of us will go through. Yours might include being bullied at school or your parents splitting up, being overly criticized on your exam results by your dad or experiencing rejection by your friendship group.

The thing about trauma is, it can stay with you. Multiple little 't's add up to create negative beliefs about ourself and the world. And those beliefs impact how we think, feel and behave. If you've been feeling stuck, helpless or unworthy, trauma could be why. The good news is, it doesn't have to stay that way.

Throughout this book, and particularly in the next chapters, you'll find tools and strategies for healing the past and regaining your lost confidence.

Summary

★ There are specific pressures and challenges that we as women have to overcome – about our appearance and the traditional roles expected of a woman – but it is possible!

★ Trauma can be healed, even if it relates to something that happened long ago.

CHAPTER 2

It's time for a change

To start off, I'm going to tell you something that may surprise you: confidence is overrated. What really counts is to dig down deeper than confidence. Because it's rediscovering your bravery that will create the foundation for true confidence, the kind that goes beyond faking it until you make it.

If confidence is having faith in yourself, bravery or being courageous is the ability to do something that frightens you. Being brave means having the willingness to try, to do your best and give things a go. It means acting even when it feels scary or uncomfortable.

Many people who appear to have been born with confidence, and seem to breeze through every challenge, still struggle internally with self-doubt. What looks impressive or easy on the outside isn't the whole story.

In *Brave New Girl*, we'll be going deep into the reasons that you've held yourself back, with plenty of inspirational stories from real women like you, who've overcome their fears to develop their confidence. You've no doubt looked at successful women who appear to have it all going on and thought, 'It's so easy for her.' But we only see the confident exterior, not what's going on inside. Adele has been known to projectile vomit before her mind-blowingly brilliant performances. Despite looking so self-assured during her 2011 TED Talk, motivational guru Mel Robbins has described feeling on the verge of a panic attack the whole way through. Speaker and uber-successful global business coach Marie Forleo has confessed to getting nervous before every single talk she does, no matter how small the audience. Even superstar Rihanna has reportedly sought coaching for confidence.

Confidence can be like a mirage: it looks great from a distance, but on closer inspection, it's hot air, simply a way of behaving. What's actually going on underneath the surface of someone who's putting themselves out there, is bravery.

Being brave doesn't mean having an absence of fear. Rather, it's being firm in the face of fear or challenges, despite the way you're feeling. Once you learn you can handle moving out of your comfort zone, real confidence starts to emerge. Confidence comes from experience.

That means you will only discover the extent of your abilities when you give something scary, hard or uncomfortable a go. It's not about being good at that thing, doing it perfectly, or getting people's approval. It's about trying and knowing that, no matter if you fall or fail or make a fool of yourself, you'll be OK. In fact, you'll be more than OK because you'll know you're BRAVE.

Being brave doesn't have to mean jumping out of an aeroplane, swimming with sharks or speaking in front of a thousand people (though it might). When we're afraid, we're brave for merely showing up.

Brave is pushing the boundaries of what has kept you small, even if only by an inch. It's poking your head around the door of what's possible for you. It's taking baby steps forward and noticing that fear shrinks when you walk towards it. Brave might mean striking up a conversation with a sales assistant in a shop, it might mean letting your sister know how she's treating you isn't OK, or going to a party and staying for just twenty minutes. Whatever is on the edge of your comfort zone will exercise your bravery and so grow your confidence.

The root of all confidence

If you think all this bravery stuff is a step too far, or if you're about to throw this book across the other side of the room and hide behind the sofa, or if you want to dismiss it as 'too much like hard work', I feel for you. This work is hard, I won't deny it.

When a challenge seems impossible, it's easy to dismiss our bold dreams or convince ourselves that they're not that important. But stay with me. In this book, I will be holding your hand and taking you step by step through the discomfort and out the other side.

We won't be jumping in at the deep end here – that might just be enough to put you off for life! Instead, we'll be implementing what Caroline Paul, author of *The Gutsy Girl*, calls 'micro-bravery'. That means small, simple steps that infuse you with self-belief, grow your confidence and, eventually, leave you feeling unstoppable.

Building your assertiveness in these small ways will strengthen you for the bigger stuff. Learn to do the little things – as small as asking your masseuse to go easy on your sore calf muscles rather than keeping quiet and wincing in pain – and you will eventually learn to do the bigger ones. That includes things as big as speaking out about discrimination at work, or standing up to the doctor who's compromising your mother's care in the hospital.

I'm going to teach you how to practise bravery. I'm going to help you push through the discomfort, and speak up. You'll learn how to do the hard things, for your benefit and for others too.

If this still sounds alien to you, remember you've already developed your confidence in so many ways. You weren't born

being confident at walking – you pulled yourself up, courageously gave it a try, fell over lots and finally learned how to
confidently toddle over to Mum or Dad. Perhaps driving or
riding a bike were once scary and new, but you now do them
on autopilot.

Every time you are brave, you'll learn assertiveness and
develop confidence. Finally, you'll be able to access and use
your potential to the full. You'll be free to try, to do your best
and to give yourself the best chance of success. And you'll
free up your energy to become authentically you.

Summary

★ Confidence comes from being brave and taking
  action.
★ Micro-bravery is about taking small steps to challenge
  yourself and grow your confidence.
★ Building your assertiveness in small ways gives you
  strength and confidence to do bigger things. It's like
  exercising a muscle.

CHAPTER 3

Believe you can change

If you're wondering how you'll ever change the shy or anxious habits of a lifetime, take heart. All of us are capable of pretty radical change. You might have heard about the concept of brain plasticity; it's the idea that the structure of our brain is always changing. All the time, you're making new neural connections and old ones are fading away. Your brain is adapting and transforming its structure according to what you do. I repeat, your brain (and therefore your skills, smarts and abilities) is flexible.

This belief that we can change is what Carol Dweck, Professor of Psychology at Stanford University, has dubbed the 'growth mindset'. It's knowing that with effort and attention, we can learn, improve and get better.

Sadly, what many of us have instead is a 'fixed mindset'. This is the belief that our qualities, such as intelligence or talents, are set and there isn't much we can do to change them. The fixed mindset keeps us stuck. It's when we believe that if we don't have a natural ability for something, we never will. It's saying to yourself, 'I'm terrible at public speaking and that's just the way it is.' Or, 'I'm not a strong person and I never will be.' Or, 'I've been shy since school and I can't see that changing.'

The truth is, for almost every skill, we will improve and learn with attention, practice and effort. And this is most definitely true for skills such as resilience, inner strength and confidence.

Instead of resigning yourself to always being the good girl

who keeps quiet about her own needs, know that you can learn confidence. Accept that with focus, you can stop caring about what people think so much, and develop the skills needed to stand up for yourself and be more assertive.

Over the course of this book, you'll feel yourself change, as you develop and reinforce your growth mindset. When it doesn't go exactly to plan, be assured you'll still be learning. In an interview with *The Atlantic*, Carol said: 'Learning something new, something hard, sticking to things—that's how you get smarter. Setbacks and feedback aren't about your abilities, they are information you could use to help yourself learn.'[1]

While you're reading and doing the exercises, you'll be growing and changing. You'll be amazed at how putting your attention on this area will see you improve in leaps and bounds. I'm excited for you to see what's possible.

. . . .

Exercise: recognize you're always learning

What have you learned lately? What new skills have you developed? Perhaps you recently changed from using an iPhone to an Android and got the hang of it in a matter of hours, or you had to get used to a new piece of software at work, or you learned the rules of a board game so well, you could teach others. Make a mental note of the ways you've learned new things and developed your skills recently.

. . . .

Own your 'why'

What will changing mean to you and your life? Remembering why you're going on this journey to confidence will help you to stay strong when what I'm asking you to do feels hard. Your 'why' is likely connected to something bigger than yourself; a dream you have or a source of meaning or purpose. It's the fuel for your internal fire.

When things feel tough – and they will – knowing your 'why' will be a powerful source of energy and inspiration to keep going. If you have to piss a few people off or move out of your comfort zone in the process, then so be it – because you know it's all worth it.

My client Anna, twenty-six, an assistant at a marketing agency, was desperate to overcome her fear of public speaking. I asked her why this was important for her. At first, she said being able to pitch her ideas to clients would help her to win new business, get promoted and earn more money. But so far, all those reasons hadn't motivated her to push through the discomfort of having all eyes on her.

I've found making more money is often not motivating in itself, it's what the money gives people that truly inspires them. When I dug deeper, asked Anna her reasons for wanting more money, her true 'why' emerged. She told me the money would give her more freedom and more opportunities for travel in her life.

She also said overcoming her fear of public speaking would give her more confidence in her relationships, she'd feel a sense of achievement at having surpassed her expectations, and – this meant a lot to her – she'd be able to use her voice and platform to help and inspire her clients.

So Anna's 'why' for public speaking boiled down to: 'Having the freedom to travel and being able to help and inspire others.' Knowing this was way more motivating and interesting to her than money alone. Finally, connecting to her 'why' gave her the courage and momentum to take action.

Your 'why' might be:

- Learning and growing so I can reach my potential and make the best of this precious life.
- Being an amazing role model for my daughter and showing her what a strong woman looks like.
- Being brave so I can be a source of inspiration for others in my work.
- Overcoming my anxiety and depression to live the best life I can.
- Having a successful business to create more freedom and fun in my life.

. . . .

Exercise: **write your mission statement**

Focus on your 'why' to create your mission statement. For one, why are you reading this book? Think about these areas too: Why you want to grow. Why you want to stand up for yourself. Why you want to carve out more time for you. Why you want to be braver.

Summary

★ Your brain is always changing and adapting; learning new skills and behaviours is always possible.
★ Remembering why you want to be more brave and confident will motivate and inspire you to transform.

PART TWO

How to learn to listen to your own voice

CHAPTER 4

Freeing yourself from what other people think

In my twenties, I'd be very wary of new people, worrying hugely what they thought of me, both at work and socially. I'd tense up and hold myself back, scared to say the wrong thing, inadvertently upset them or come across as 'too much'. I felt I had to be pleasing to others, I needed to appear perfect, easy-going and calm – which is more than a little challenging for someone who is undoubtedly imperfect and kind of a control freak.

I used to feel as though the real me only came out after several G&Ts drunk in quick succession, when I could let down my defences, or when I was with friends who knew me so well we were practically family. They'd seen me at my worst and still hung around so I figured there was less chance I could horrify them with my flaws, less chance of me being abandoned.

It's true that a small amount of concern for the opinions of others can be helpful. If we gave absolutely zero fucks about other people, we might find it hard to fit in at work – and our friends might not hang around for long, either. But caring becomes a problem when it causes you to hold yourself back, not stand up for yourself and not ask for what you want and need.

The problem with filtering yourself is that when you filter out the 'bad' bits of your personality, you lose the 'good' too. When I'm concerned with what people think of me, I suppress my sense of humour, my quirks . . . my whole personality. The result? Dull. When you try to smooth your rough edges, you also dim your sparkle.

But even by holding yourself back until you're a shadow of your true self, you can't control the other person's perception of you. Research suggests people make a first impression of you within a matter of milliseconds anyway.[1] And for all you know, they might find the repressed you more annoying than the 'too much' you!

The fact is, you can't control what people think of you. The more you try by contorting yourself, the less 'you' you become. And that's a big waste of who you are. Ask yourself: Is being watered down ever a good thing?

So why do we worry so much what people think?

If we feel secure, loved and valuable within ourselves, what other people think matters less. We don't need anyone else to tell us we're good enough, and when others tell us they think we're great, we believe them. We're able to meet our own need for acceptance from within ourselves.

However, if we're doubtful, unsure or insecure about ourselves, we're more likely to seek approval from others or take criticisms to heart. And positive comments from others are less likely to stick.

The reason often goes back to experiences in our early life. How you were treated while growing up creates the blueprint for how you feel about yourself in your later life. It's like an internal script that our subconscious uses as rules for life. But there is hope; it's totally possible to change the script. Later on, I'll walk you through the steps involved in changing the stories you tell yourself and shifting your beliefs to more positive ones.

Why we need to fit in

First, it's useful to know why we feel such a strong need to fit in. Regardless of anything that may have happened in your life, all human beings need to belong. Most of us felt this most strongly in our teenage years, when having the right trainers for PE class or being up to speed with the latest telly sensation was priority number one. I mean, it felt life-or-death important. But that's because, for our ancestors, fitting in actually was.

Human beings evolved as social creatures; we thrived because of our ability to cooperate and work together in groups. For 99 per cent of the 200,000 years we've been on earth, we lived as nomadic hunter-gatherers. If a prehistoric woman was rejected by her tribe, she'd be kicked out of the community, exposed to the elements and predators – and she wouldn't have survived long. We are hard-wired to bond with the tribe. So our fear that people will reject us is a deep and primal one.

This is one reason why, for some, going on stage to give a talk, or getting into a confrontation with a colleague, can put you into full-blown fight-or-flight mode. You feel you're at risk of rejection. And because, according to evolution, rejection is life or death, the stakes feel incredibly high. In modern times, fluffing a presentation or pissing off a workmate is hardly a death sentence – but it feels that way.

As worrying what people think of us is wired into us for our survival, know you're not alone in this. And, in modern times, you can also know you're safe no matter what people think of you. Knowing both those things, now you can begin to retrain your mindset to care less so you can be free to be yourself.

. . . .

Exercise: handing over your unwanted baggage

When you care too much about what other people think of you, you are taking on a lot of other people's stuff. This guided meditation will help you begin to care less:

Close your eyes, take some deep breaths and imagine each part of your body relaxing in turn.

Imagine you're carrying a heavy rucksack. In the rucksack are all the unhelpful stories you've taken on board in your life. Recognize how they're all based on the past; you took on other people's judgements, insecurities and stress. Imagine feeling the weight of that on your shoulders. But it's all out of date and it doesn't apply to you any more. Those old stories that were designed to keep you safe – playing small, bending yourself out of shape to try to fit in, rejecting yourself before anyone else has a chance to – they're all out of date. The past is over now. It's time for a new way of thinking, feeling and responding.

Allow the rucksack to slide off one shoulder and to the ground.

Feel a sense of relief, like a weight having been lifted off your back.

. . . .

Summary

★ It's impossible to control what other people think of you; so you may as well be yourself.

★ A desire to fit in is hard-wired into all of us.

★ When you filter out the 'bad' bits of your personality, you lose the 'good' too.

CHAPTER 5

Reboot your beliefs

What you believe feels 100 per cent true. But, as I said before, it isn't. For me, uncovering my hidden beliefs was the missing piece of the puzzle. It was only when I saw clearly the thought patterns holding me back that I truly made progress in reducing my anxiety and increasing my confidence levels.

Thinking about where our beliefs come from can feel tricky. It's easy to cop out, as I did at first, and say, 'This is just the way I am,' to dismiss the reasons why you hold the beliefs you do. It can be painful to delve into the past and go back to where these ideas originated. If you love your parents, you probably can't bear the thought of them being responsible for your present unhappiness. Or perhaps you recognize you had a difficult time growing up and there's part of you that doesn't want to think about it. Either way, I promise getting clear on where these negative, old ideas came from will be empowering and ultimately hugely positive. Awareness is the first step to change. The more you understand yourself, the more you can use that information to get better.

Did your negative belief that you are not good enough come from something that happened to you in childhood? Was your belief that you should stay quiet and wait to be spoken to originally learned from your parents? From school? From a difficult experience in your work or social life?

As a child I was a mixture of hyperactive and chatty with shy and nervous. I was emotional and sensitive, prone to outbursts, tantrums and hysteria. One minute I'd be happily chatting, the next I'd be dramatically rolling around on the floor.

I was fond of expressing my extreme emotions in public places with lots of kicking and screaming. My dad, an extraordinarily calm and patient man, famed for his laid-back approach to parenting, would eventually reach the end of his tether. Exasperated, he would get down to my level and hiss, '*Stop showing me up!*'

Now, up until the age of about seven or eight, our developing brains are very much in download mode. We absorb stuff. We absorb what we're told, what we see other people doing and what we hear them saying. This is a very useful ability indeed, helping us to learn how to walk, talk, feed ourselves (and say our first swear words).

Where this ability lets us down is that, at that young age, we don't have discernment or context. We take things literally. As an hysterical five-year-old, I didn't understand Dad was doing his best. He was stressed, tired and trying to wrestle his daughter out of the frozen food aisle of Asda in one piece in time for *Neighbours*. At that moment, I didn't understand I was loved, accepted and treasured, and Dad was only acting out of his own frustration and shame. The message my young brain absorbed from this experience was: 'I am an embarrassment.'

This (and other similar experiences) meant my brain hung on to the belief I was somebody to be ashamed of. That I was 'bad', 'embarrassing', 'unworthy'. Having a young, receptive brain and no context for the fact that my dad was just tired and stressed, these messages became embedded in my subconscious.

But why on earth do people take on board beliefs that are so clearly unhelpful? The answer is again: survival. The human brain isn't designed to make you happy, its job is to keep you alive. The rapid absorption of information in childhood is to help us learn as much as possible about how to survive in the big, bad world. If a child is repeatedly told to shut up and be quiet by an angry parent, the message they receive is that being quiet is necessary for survival. If you're left waiting at the school gates for your no-show alcoholic mother to pick you up and take you back to your chaotic home, being on high alert for danger makes sense. Its role is to potentially keep you safe. And as anything involved with survival gets wired into the brain, it's no wonder this stuff can be so hard to shake in adulthood.

If the idea of blaming your parents makes you uncomfortable, know that you're not doing this exercise to blame but to recognize where your beliefs stem from. No parent is perfect and while some are certainly less perfect than others, they did their best with what they knew and the resources they had at the time. Your parents got their conditioning from their imperfect parents who got theirs from their parents . . . and so the long line of parents messing up kids continues. We are all just humans trying to do our best.

That said, negative beliefs originating in childhood are often at the root of us feeling lacking and unworthy of anything other than playing small. I'm going to call them 'unhelpful stories'; the stories that we tell ourselves that are out of date and hold us back. And these same beliefs will often show up time and time again in your life. Which ones in the list below sound familiar to you?

People will abandon me

My client Cara grew up with a father who was a workaholic. He would frequently get home from work after she'd gone to bed, and leave for work before she was up. He'd take long work trips, often for weeks at a time. Then, when Cara was twelve, her father announced he'd met someone else and left the family home. Although he was still in her life, the message she received was this: the people you love will leave you.

In an unconscious attempt to protect herself against being abandoned again, Cara learned to please others and to keep them on side by putting her own needs behind anyone else's. The result was, time and time again, she got walked all over, both at work and in relationships. She seemed to attract people who took advantage and left her feeling exhausted, needy and unworthy.

Maybe your life has a more extreme version of Cara's situation? Perhaps you were adopted or put into care or a parent died? Or perhaps your version is less obvious, such as being the middle child who didn't get as much attention as your other siblings. Whether it was a massive deal or seemingly minor, an abandonment story can have a lasting impact.

I'll be rejected

From the girl gang that stonewalled you for a week in Year 7, to the boy you fell in love with in Year 9 who only wanted to be friends, to getting fired from your first job – all rejection can leave an imprint and make us warier. We take rejection personally, make it mean something about us, that we're unworthy or unlovable.

If your mind constantly plays you a story that you always get passed up, you will find yourself gravitating towards situations to fit that narrative. A rejection story could mean you're attracted to the bad boys or girls, or else you've taken yourself out of the love game completely, to ensure you'll never even have a chance to be rejected. Perhaps you were rejected a few times in the past but now, if you're honest, you are putting yourself down first before anyone else has a chance to.

The truth is, often the original rejection probably had little to do with us and much more to do with the other person's preferences, issues or stress. But now our brain, always trying to keep us safe and protect us, is hyper-aware of any sign of rejection.

I'm not good enough

My client Andrea told me, 'My mum was often sad. I'd get home to find her crying at the kitchen table. Sometimes she wouldn't get out of bed for days. I thought if I could be a really good girl, maybe Mum would be happier.

'I worked hard to be the perfect child, to get the best marks at school, look after my younger brothers and try to help wherever I could. Even so, Mum stayed depressed. Nothing I did made a difference. I now know her depression was not my fault, but at the time I believed it was, and never felt I was doing enough.'

Maybe you had a critical parent for whom nothing was ever up to standard, or your family prized achievement above all and you always felt you were failing? Ali, twenty-three, an ex-drama school student, credits the competitive environment there for her adult belief that she's always falling short. Students were pitted against each other and the competition to be the prettiest, the slimmest and the most charismatic was ever present. Even though Ali has left the acting world behind, she has retained the unhelpful story that she could never be good enough.

I don't belong

Many people have a deep fear that they don't fit in. As I said before, a sense of belonging is essential to us as human beings and not fitting in can feel like life or death, especially in our early and teenage years. In fact, in the key psychological theory, Maslow's hierarchy of needs, 'love and belonging' is the third most important level, coming right after 'physical needs' and 'safety'.

If you feel you don't fit in, question where that belief may have come from. For me, it was about having a different accent to everyone at school. My parents were from the south of England and I went to school in the north. On top of that, my nickname was 'hippy' or 'freak' because my family was veggie. For you, your belief may have come from the fact you preferred books growing up while others liked TV, or you were a different ethnicity, sexual orientation or religion to the majority around you. You might have been singled out or judged. Perhaps you were told you were different and you have never shaken off that label.

It might be that you genuinely are different to many of the people around you, due to the colour of your skin or your sexual orientation. Or there might be smaller differences that still seem like a big deal to you: the fact that you love tarot cards while most of your peers love Netflix and beer, or you love R&B while most of your mates listen to EDM. Your job is to realize that that is OK. While you can't control what other people think of you, you can control your own sense of belonging and start to decondition the negative programming you have received in your life. Can you start to label your differences as unique and special features instead? Because the truth is that we all do belong.

. . . .

Exercise: **your old story vs your new one**

In this exercise, start to uncover all the old stories and beliefs that have held you back. Think of situations that affected you. What meaning were you giving each situation? What story are you telling yourself? Can you think of another possible explanation that can become your new story? For example:

What happened	Old story	New story
My dad left when I was twelve.	I made it mean that I am unlovable and will be abandoned. It means I developed a pattern of neediness and of people pleasing.	Dad left for his own reasons that have nothing to do with me or how much he loved me. Many other people love me and have stuck around.

. . . .

Exercise: **talk to your negative beliefs**

Think about yourself as made up of different parts, with one of them the part that feels they don't belong, aren't good enough or will be abandoned. It can be helpful to think of this part as a separate character or person.

Step 1: Imagine the part of you that's responsible for the feeling of being rejected as a character or version of you. What does she look like? How does she act? What does she want? How is she trying to help you?

For example, I have a part of me that feels separate, left out and that doesn't belong. She looks like me aged fourteen – tall and skinny, with glasses and braces. She's awkward, shy and ashamed. She's desperately trying to help me fit in, by being accommodating, meek and keeping quiet so she doesn't stand out. She's trying to keep me safe from feeling embarrassed or getting rejected.

Step 2: Thank this part for what she's been trying to do. Let her know how grateful you are that she's been trying to keep you safe for so long. Then explain to her that what she's doing isn't needed any more. Tell her that she's operating on old information, that she's not in secondary school (or wherever is relevant) any more. Tell her everything you love about her. Give her a big hug and some words of reassurance.

Step 3: Next imagine another part of you. This part is strong, confident and knows her worth. I like to imagine mine mixed with a dash of Beyoncé and a hint of Wonder Woman. She's standing tall, holding her head up high and exuding confidence and self-esteem. Now imagine the old part merging into your new part and the whole becoming even more empowered. Let this new part take over and imagine acting, thinking and speaking from a place of confidence.

· ·

Summary

★ Your beliefs often have their roots in childhood. In the present, they impact your thoughts and feelings.

★ The first step is to identify the belief – then you can start to write a new story for yourself.

CHAPTER 6

Debug your thinking

As human beings, we're all prone to ways of thinking irrationally. We all have common but unhelpful thought patterns that trip us up. Questioning these patterns is another way to help unhook yourself from excessive worrying about what other people think. In fact, just becoming aware of them is the first step in freeing yourself. Which of these 'thinking errors' can you spot in your own thinking?

Mind-reading

I bet you thought mind-reading was impossible, right? Well it is, but that doesn't stop many of us, sometimes even on a daily basis, believing we can do it. In the past, I've been a brilliant mind-reader – I could interpret the most inconclusive body language or tone of voice as a sign the other person 'hates me'. Not replying to my texts right away? I've done something to upset you. Yawning while I'm speaking to you? I must be a massive bore. The drama! When we read minds, we almost never assume the good stuff but instead the catastrophically negative and critical.

A close cousin of mind-reading is projection, where we fling our own thoughts and beliefs on to the other person. You feel insecure about what you're wearing that day, so you project that and believe they must be judging you for it. Usually, the only person judging you is you. A subcategory of mind-reading is 'jumping to conclusions'. You pick up on the slightest, practically imperceptible, facial expression and then conclude the other person is annoyed with you.

Generalizations

'No one likes me, everyone is good at speaking up in meetings except for me, I always end up making a fool of myself.' Sound familiar? If you're prone to overgeneralizing, you're distorting the world in an irrational and untrue way. What do you mean 'no one likes me' – what, no one, ever, in the history of liking, has ever liked you? Have you always made a fool of yourself? Every. Single. Time? Has there never been a time when you didn't make a fool of yourself?

Put like this, we start to see how silly our generalizations really are. My client Reena told me, 'My boyfriend always blames me for all our arguments.' But on closer questioning, it turned out sometimes he did take responsibility and she blamed him a fair bit too. Keep an ear out for clues: often it's using words such as 'always', 'never', 'everyone', 'nobody' and 'everything'. And recognize that to generalize is irrational, and so any conclusions are untrue.

Black and white thinking

'If it's not perfect, it's a failure.'
  'If one person dislikes me, I'm a loser.'
  'If I don't agree with everything, he'll abandon me.'
  Our brains like to categorize things into black/white, good/

bad because it's simpler, but this is never how it works in the real world. Everything is on a continuum. There are always shades of grey.

Filtering out the good stuff, only hearing the negative

Shout out to everyone who has her gloom-tinted glasses on. You walk out of a six-month review where 95 per cent of the discussion was positive . . . yet your mind stays fixated on the 5 per cent that was critical. So much so that the glowing feedback goes right over your head. This is down to 'negativity bias', our natural inclination to remember the negative over the positive (it's another one of those evolutionary survival mechanisms). Being aware of negative bias means we know to work harder to cling to the good stuff.

Personalization

Your mum is struggling with depression – and it's all your fault. The company you work for lost money this year – and it's because you didn't work hard enough. Your best friend must be mad at you – because she hasn't replied to your last three messages. You're taking life too personally, feeling guilt and responsibility for things that aren't really your fault, in fact may have nothing to do with you.

Shoulds and musts

'I should be further ahead in my career.'

'I should have this sorted at my age.'

'I must be more confident.'

Why should you? According to who or what? Many of us 'should' all over ourselves, basing these 'shoulds' on arbitrary and meaningless standards. This is not helpful or constructive, and it holds us back from being ourselves and doing what we'd love to do.

Confirmation bias

We search for evidence to support our beliefs. Even when the evidence is lacking, we'll find it, or when it's unclear we'll misinterpret it to fit in with what we believe is true. For example, if you believe you're not intelligent enough, your brain will hone in on all the ways you're not smart and ignore all the ways you are. Or if you believe no one could ever be attracted to you, you'll become blind to the person who's flirting with you.

. . . .

Exercise: be a bias detective

Notice where in your life you tend to experience these errors and biases in your thinking. Recognize some of the common thoughts you have and write them down. Then question them. Is this true always? Never? Why *should* you? According to who? For example:

Negative thought	Thinking error	Rational, kind perspective
I lost my train of thought in the presentation and it completely ruined it.	Black and white thinking, generalization and mind-reading.	I got good feedback after the presentation and most of it went well. I don't need to be perfect in order to be good. Some people told me it went well. I can't read minds so I can't know what everyone else was thinking.

Summary

★ As human beings, we're prone to thinking errors such as generalizing and taking things personally.

★ Identifying your thinking errors will help to stop them from tripping you up.

CHAPTER 7

Meet your inner imposter

Writing my first book, *The Anxiety Solution*, was relatively easy for me. I knew what I wanted to say and how I wanted to say it and I wrote it in a matter of months without any drama. However, three weeks before publication (and the irony is not lost on me) I started to feel hugely uneasy, anxious even, about the prospect of my book being out in the world. Who was I to write a book about anxiety? What did I know? I wasn't perfect and I didn't have all the answers. Surely anyone off the street would know more about anxiety than me?! Suddenly, I'd gone from Kanye West-level confidence to a skydiver about to jump for the first time. I visualized one-star Amazon reviews, pitying looks from my friends and piles of my book marked 'reduced to clear' in the pound shop.

If you've ever felt like a fraud who's going to be 'found out' at any moment, don't worry, you're in good company. Emma Watson, Kate Winslet, Sheryl Sandberg and even Meryl Streep have confessed they share your plight.

Emma Watson describes it like this: 'It's almost like the better I do, the more my feeling of inadequacy actually increases, because I'm just going, any moment, someone's going to find out I'm a total fraud, and that I don't deserve any of what I've achieved. I can't possibly live up to what everyone thinks I am and what everyone's expectations of me are.'[1]

The first step to getting in control of something is to define it. And guys, this particular brand of self-doubt even has a name: 'imposter syndrome'. IT'S A SYNDROME! It's a real thing. I for one feel so much better knowing it's a recognized issue, experienced by millions, i.e. not just you and me.

Imposter syndrome dogs successful women in particular – even more so if you're a minority in your place of work, for example if you're a woman in a male-dominated industry. But in fact, it's just another way that our old friend fear pops up to make itself known. As COO of Facebook, Sheryl Sandberg is at a career pinnacle and undoubtedly incredibly successful – but she has described having textbook imposter syndrome. As she puts it in her book, *Lean In*: 'Fear is at the root of so many of the barriers that women face. Fear of not being liked. Fear of making the wrong choice. Fear of drawing negative attention. Fear of overreaching. Fear of being judged. Fear of failure.'

She goes on to say: 'Every time I was called on in class, I was sure that I was about to embarrass myself. Every time I took a test, I was sure that it had gone badly. And every time I didn't embarrass myself – or even excelled – I believed that I had fooled everyone yet again. One day soon, the jig would be up.'

A classic sign of imposter syndrome is writing off your successes as luck. You've been blagging it all this time, haven't you!? You bluffed your way to a 2:1 at uni, you winged the job interview, managed to fool everyone at work for five years that you aren't a chancer . . . oh, and that you have any friends at all is purely blind luck too!

The downsides of imposter syndrome are real: when we feel like a fraud, we're less likely to accept praise, ask for help, go for the promotion and take risks. It holds us back and damages our peace of mind. It puts you at risk of burnout, depression and slower progression in your career.

The good news is, once you've named imposter syndrome, you can tame it. You can call it out for the prevalent and insidious affliction that it is. Once you have recognized it and brought your awareness to it, you suddenly have a choice about how you respond.

There is more good news. In the same way as if you worry about being a psychopath, you definitely aren't one (a true psychopath wouldn't worry), if you're concerned you might be an 'imposter', chances are you aren't. Phew! A person who really is a fraud wouldn't worry about it.

One reason why you may have taken on this pattern of self-doubt is to appear relatable and likeable, not to appear arrogant or over-confident. You may have seen it modelled by other women. In our culture, confident women can be labelled bossy bitches. And right now, being liked is more important for women than men. At Tina Brown's Women in the World Summit, Hillary Clinton said what many studies have suggested: 'With men, success and ambition are correlated with likability, so the more successful a man is, the more likeable he becomes. With a woman, guess what? It's the exact opposite.'

You also might feel that questioning your abilities offers some kind of protection against making mistakes. Not only is that not true, but when the social pressure to downplay our abilities and appear modest takes hold, we appear less confident and capable to others, which can end up hindering our career progression. And the more we do it, the more we believe we are unworthy.

Even women who are highly trained and at the top of their profession experience imposter syndrome. I spoke to several doctors who told me it's rife amongst women in the medical profession. My friend Rosie, a 33-year-old anaesthetist, said, 'In recent months, three of my highly respected female consultants have confessed to moments of imposter syndrome.'

Arguably, in certain professions – including medicine – having a healthy level of self-doubt is useful. Imposter syndrome can keep us learning and striving to be better. But once it starts to hold us back, it's gone too far. Ask yourself: is this self-doubt serving me? Because if you're crippled by it, if it stops you from making decisions, progressing in your career or leading in the way you'd like to, it's time to change. Some suggestions of where to begin: start to trust and appreciate yourself more and to give your support to other confident women.

. . . .

Exercise: where are you dumbing down?

Reflect on these questions:

Are you dumbing down your abilities in order to appear more likeable?

In what ways and when?

If so, is doing this really serving you?

. . . .

Exercise: how you made it all happen

It's important to recognize your achievements are not all 'just luck', but that you are capable, resourceful and talented. Your hard work, your ability to build your network and your intelligence made your successes happen. If you've been putting your success down to fluke, it's time to look at the facts and start giving yourself a bit more credit. In her book *The Coach's Casebook* Kim Morgan includes this great exercise:

Write down a timeline of your career, identifying each achievement and success. Crucially, also include details of how you made each one happen.

Which of your qualities made that achievement possible?

What does that success say about you?

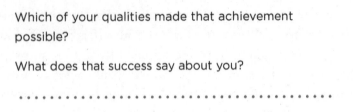

How to reframe your imposterhood

During the period of anxiety before my book was released, I had to give myself a serious talking to (or more than one). Every time I thought, 'Who am I to do this?' I replaced it with, 'Who am I not to do this? If not me, then who?' No one else could have written this exact book, it had to be me! I had to own my imperfections, accept I didn't know everything (and that was OK) and start to appreciate the value and experience that I did have to offer.

You could try this reframe: 'If you don't have imposter syndrome, are you even doing it right?' Think of imposter syndrome as a sign you're moving outside your comfort zone. You're growing. You're stretching. You're making progress. And if imposter syndrome has to come along for the ride, so be it.

Or try this one. If you've been asking yourself, 'Why me? Who am I to do this?' replace it with what actress and comedian Mindy Kaling famously tweeted about imposter syndrome: 'Why the fuck not me?!'[2]

And finally, remember that some of the most impressive people don't feel 100 per cent qualified – but charge ahead anyway. Richard Branson wrote: 'If somebody offers you an amazing opportunity but you are not sure you can do it, say yes – then learn how to do it later!' What do all successful women with imposter syndrome have in common? They take action, regardless of any doubts. They make a start, even if they don't feel ready. They experience the thoughts but they don't take them seriously enough to let them stop them. They feel the fear – but they do it anyway.

Donna, twenty-seven, an entrepreneur, told me, 'When I first started freelancing and carving out my own career I suffered with imposter syndrome pretty much every day. There were some days when it took over. The little comments people threw my way, "You're very young!" or, "How do you know how to run a business?" or, "Shouldn't you be working full time?" would repeat over and over in my head. I focused a lot of energy on what other people were doing rather than concentrating on my business and talents. It's been four years now since I started out on my own and I doubt imposter syndrome will ever totally disappear for me. But I know how to keep the imposter monster at bay by constantly reminding myself to stay in my own lane, to keep doing what I believe in and to focus on how good that feels.'

. . . .

Exercise: **mutual admiration**

Contact five friends and colleagues and ask them to tell you what they admire about you and what they believe are your strengths. You may cringe at the thought of doing this (I did at first) but trust me, it's incredibly powerful. You can return the favour and let them know what you admire about them in the process, for mutual admiration. It's a beautiful way to tell people the reasons you appreciate, love and admire them while getting some positive feedback yourself. Warning: this exercise will move you – and others – to tears.

. . . .

. . . .

Exercise: three steps to overcoming imposter syndrome

1. *Self-compassion.* Feeling like an imposter is incredibly common amongst successful women, so you're in good company. Having compassion for yourself, in the same way you would for a friend who's struggling, is key. Remind yourself that feeling like an imposter is a sign you're moving out of your comfort zone. Growth can be uncomfortable, but it's a good thing. Accept it's OK to have these thoughts and feelings. Be as gentle with yourself as you can.

2. *Examine the proof.* What is the evidence that you are indeed capable and good enough? Think back through your life and career and note the successes, progress and impact you've had. Remind yourself how you made each one happen.

3. *Do the thing.* Say to yourself, 'Oh hi, Imposter Syndrome. I see you. But I'm taking action anyway.' Action is the most potent way to prove your self-doubts wrong. You show yourself just what your abilities are. And even if things don't go to plan, you're learning important information to help you improve later. If you're feeling like an imposter, remember that if you're 'doing the thing', you are in fact the real deal. You're doing it!

. . . .

Summary

★ Feeling like a fraud is incredibly common, especially in successful women.

★ Instead of putting your successes down to luck, remember what it was about you that made each thing happen.

CHAPTER 8

Learn to love compliments

Why is it so hard to accept a compliment? I confess I've batted back a fair few in my time. Maybe you've discounted what someone said about your new dress, 'It's five years old!' Or argued back, 'It makes my love handles look HUGE though, doesn't it?' Or scrambled to compliment *them*, 'No, *your* dress is incredible.' Or my personal (least) fave, simply got embarrassed, changed the subject and so ignored they ever said anything nice (yeah, sorry about that #rude).

We reject compliments out of hand from embarrassment and from trying to be modest, plus a side order of thinking, 'They're just saying it to be nice.' A 2017 study found people have difficulty accepting compliments when we don't believe the other person is being sincere[1] . . . which is often due to low self-esteem. If a compliment doesn't fit in with our internal image of ourselves, we might think, 'They're just saying that!' Or, 'What does she know?' This can make a compliment backfire, as it highlights and worsens how unsuccessful we feel we are. But think about this: even if someone is only complimenting you to be nice, they're doing it because they want you to like them – which is actually a pretty amazing compliment in itself.

Many of us feel we must appear modest and are scared of appearing arrogant or conceited. Often, we're conditioned like this from an early age. I was raised to believe being modest, listening more than speaking, and not 'showing off' were key when it came to being liked. Messages from parents or teachers along these lines often came from a place of love or concern (although it's true some people do trample on you to elevate their own self-esteem). But when we internalize them, take them too far, it can result in us holding ourselves back and covering up our most sparkly selves.

Also, have you ever thought how batting away compliments can have the opposite effect to the one you'd intended? Because when you reject compliments, you either seem ungracious or, worse, as though you're fishing for more!

Accepting compliments also makes the giver feel good. If you snap back that you don't agree that your coat is ah-may-zing and that, in fact, it's old or unloved or unstylish, you're actually dissing their taste. Being given a compliment is like being given a gift – would you throw a gift back in their face and tell them it's a worthless piece of shit? No! That would be rude (also, you love gifts, remember!?).

Try to accept a compliment graciously, trusting it comes from a good place in the other person. Doing this has been shown to help you to be mentally healthy. A Japanese study found praise can improve performance, and compliments can also boost your mood, your confidence and your level of motivation.[2]

Recognize your human need to feel appreciated. Give yourself permission to receive. When you're being given good feedback or praise, listen with openness, take a deep breath and let it sink in. Make a mental note and reflect back on it often. I've learned to treasure the compliments I've received, and some of them I love to think about. Keeping them in mind can work as an antidote to the self-flagellation many of us subject ourselves to, act as balm for our self-esteem, a shield against negative self-talk and help stop us taking external criticism to heart.

. . . .

Exercise: **fill up your compliment bank**

Mentally review all the friends, family, partners and bosses you've had in your life. As you do, make a list of every compliment each one has given you and every good bit of feedback you've received. Save the list somewhere you can review it often – and particularly when you're stuck in imposter syndrome or self-doubt.

. . . .

Exercise: **alien appreciation**

Most of us are conditioned to spot our own flaws. When we measure ourselves against the filtered perfection of Instagram stars, our own less-than-perfect forms can seem starkly lacking.

We're often much harsher on ourselves than we are on anyone else. I noticed this recently when sitting opposite a woman on the train. I admired her interesting personal style, wearing a checked shirt and boyfriend jeans, the comfortable way she held herself, and her hair that fell artlessly just below her shoulders. She didn't look polished and she didn't fit with the constructed idea of perfection that society has created. But she was beautiful and I could appreciate her attractiveness in a way I couldn't my own.

It made me think of all the times I've only been able to see my flaws. And reminded me of how easily our self-perception can become warped, due to our own low self-esteem and when reflected by the media and social media.

In this exercise, I'd like you to start to see yourself the way a (friendly) alien would. To this alien, without a frame of comparison or perfection, everything is equally beautiful and amazing – every colour, shape, size and texture is incredible.

Imagine coming to earth with these fresh eyes and seeing yourself as if for the first time. View yourself with the same awe and admiration as you would a rare and beautiful animal. The next time you catch yourself grabbing your belly fat in despair or lamenting your pore size (I mean, how ridiculous that this is even a thing), can you hold this frame of reference in your mind?

Summary

★ Make a conscious effort to accept compliments graciously.

★ Remember all the compliments and good feedback you've been given. Review them regularly.

CHAPTER 9

Say goodbye, inner critic

November 2017 was a high point of my career. For years I'd had it in my mind that I wanted to speak at Stylist Live in London. After the success of my first book, *The Anxiety Solution*, I was finally invited to give a talk there. I was well prepared and as I strolled on to the stage, sporting my headset microphone (feeling not unlike Britney Spears) I felt calm, confident and excited.

Only two weeks earlier, it had been a totally different story. I'm a self-confessed self-improvement junkie and my search for inner peace has taken me from India to Bali to Guatemala and back. But that time, I'd found myself in Northern Ibiza, at a retreat for women designed to help us to calm our minds and heal our past pain. The White Isle may have a reputation for parties of the retox variety, but yoga, meditation and green juice aficionados head to the north to get their fix of wellness.

For five days, we'd be honing our downward dogs, quieting our monkey minds with meditation and sharing our deepest inner experiences in a circle. While I'm now confident at public speaking, sharing off the cuff in a circle about the struggles I was experiencing brought up old fears I thought I'd left behind. I'm used to being the 'expert' who people come to hear; I prepare beforehand and what I share is therefore often well rehearsed. But this was different. If you dread having to go around the table and introduce yourself in a meeting, you'll relate to my mounting fear each time my turn to speak grew closer, that familiar shaky, heart-thumping anxiety. Then, as I spoke, I'd mentally question everything I said, berating myself simultaneously for not being good enough and not confident enough.

A few days into the trip, while I was gazing at a cactus against the blue sky, wondering what on earth I was doing there (and considering making a run for it!), I had a realization. The only person judging me, was me. I didn't think the things I had to say were interesting enough. I didn't believe I had the right to speak up. I was the one who thought what I was sharing sounded stupid. No one else cared. In fact, my rational mind knew this group of women to be amongst the most kind and accepting people I'd ever met. All the criticism was coming from my inner critic, my own worst enemy.

Once I realized all of this, I knew I had to give myself a break. I told myself, 'I have nothing to prove to anyone.' I reaffirmed it was OK to feel vulnerable, to be imperfect, to feel scared.

I've since learned that before it's my turn to share in a circle, I need to take a deep breath and to allow my awareness to sink into my body. I focus on my stomach (there are a lot of neurones – nerve cells – in the gut, aka the 'second brain'). And I trust that whatever comes out of my mouth will be what's right and true for me at that moment.

The soundtrack to your life

Your inner critic loves to pipe up, especially when you're in new or challenging situations. If you listen, you might even hear it giving you a running commentary on everything you say and do, chipping in with its hurtful and destructive narrative.

By now, I hope you understand that the person who has the most capacity to hurt you, is you. It's you who gives your inner critic all the power. The only person whose judgement really stings, is your own. If you know you're a hard worker and someone calls you lazy, it's easy to let it go because it doesn't fit with your self-image. But if you have a deep fear that you're lazy (maybe even despite the evidence) it will hurt, because there's already a wound there. When we heal these wounds and start to love and accept ourselves, what other people think of us becomes less and less important.

. . . .

Exercise: a letter to your inner critic

I've named my inner critic Angelica, after the mean little girl from *Rugrats*. I suggest you give yours a character too, complete with a silly voice. It could be from a film or TV show, or one you make up. This will help you to distance yourself from the unwanted inner voice, to take it less seriously. Now write her a letter, thanking her for what she's been trying to do and letting her know it's time to part ways. This is my example:

Dear Angelica,

I see you. I know what you've been trying to do. I know you've been trying to help me. I know your perfectionism and criticism is because you've been trying to make me 'better'. I see you've been trying to protect me; from failure, from the judgement of others. But when you put me down, it hurts just as much as someone else doing it (possibly more). And you're holding me back from what I really want.

Thanks for what you've been trying to do, but it's time for us to say goodbye. I've outgrown you now. Perfection is a myth and I don't need you to protect me any more. I'm putting you on the shelf and, from now on, I'm not letting you interfere with my life or hold me back.

Summary

★ Everyone has an inner critic, but you get to decide whether to believe yours or not.

★ The only person whose judgement can really hurt you, is you.

PART THREE

How to stop apologizing for yourself – and say NO

CHAPTER 10

Shatter the illusion of perfectionism

In a world of plastic surgery, pore-blurring primer, air-brush phone filters and spell checkers, flaws and mistakes can feel unacceptable. It seems fairly ridiculous written down, but what we often do is compare ourselves to the idea of a perfect woman. This is a lose-lose game. It goes back to our deep-seated fear that if we show weakness or vulnerability, we won't be liked or accepted.

It isn't clear exactly why but research shows women are more likely to be perfectionists than men.[1] Possible underlying reasons include our higher self-doubt, our lower self-esteem and more pressure to look perfect from the media. Evidence from Girlguiding UK found that girls as young as seven feel the pressure to be perfect, with 38 per cent feeling they're not pretty enough.[2]

If you have a messy desk or thousands of unopened emails, you might assume there's no way you're a perfectionist. But perfectionism can show up in ways that are less obvious, such as fear of being disliked for your choices, for what you say or how you look. You might avoid doing anything that risks making you look silly, or anything you're a beginner at, or you might be highly critical of yourself or others.

Alternatively, you may not think you're a perfectionist because you're not aceing it. Nicola, twenty-four, a buying assistant, told me: 'I always thought you had to be an over-achiever to be a perfectionist. But I'm the opposite: I hate myself for anything less than perfect so I don't even try or start. I underachieve, I procrastinate. I'm cautious, very self-critical and socially anxious because I think other people are being critical of my flaws the way I am too.' Being a perfectionist is corrosive to confidence because it can mean we hold ourselves back so we never have the chance to be seen to try, and fail.

Perfectionism is a form of black and white thinking. You can be perfect or a failure; there's no in between. You either get 100 per cent good feedback on your project or it was a disaster. You either feel your make-up is flawless or your slightly uneven eyeliner is all you can see. Perfectionism discounts the good, great, interesting, fine and wonderfully imperfect things that lie in between. What sucks the most about being a perfectionist is it trains your mind to be highly critical, to keep searching for flaws – and so you'll always find one.

Becky, thirty-seven, told me: 'If my hair didn't look exactly as I wanted, or if my outfit didn't match with the picture in my head, then the whole day or night would be ruined. This could also extend to wanting the DIY I did on my house to look perfect (which is hilarious because I'm terrible at DIY), or wanting to be the best at work so no one could ever tell me I'd done something wrong.'

In the past, I felt huge pressure to appear perfect. I thought if I did and said all the right things, people would like and accept me. I didn't want to upset or annoy anyone for fear of being criticized or judged. Being disliked was unacceptable.

If I knew someone didn't like me, it would sting for days. If I didn't think I looked good, it would taint the whole day, as I fixated on what I saw as my defects. Doing or saying the 'wrong' thing (whatever that meant) or appearing overly vulnerable also terrified me. I felt like a mollusc with no shell, naked and delicate, desperate to hide behind a perfect facade. I denied my own vulnerability, shoved it down, put on a front of being OK. Looking back, I realize a big part of my need to appear perfect was due to shame and the fact I couldn't accept my own imperfections (we'll cover this in Chapter 18 'Find the courage to be imperfect'). Because once we really know and own all parts of ourselves, what others think becomes less important.

When you chase perfection, not only can you never reach it but, just as I did, you expend a lot of valuable energy filtering and suppressing yourself in the process. Trying to be perfect is exhausting. You can't truly be yourself and express all the interesting and unique things that make you who you are.

Human beings are messy. We sweat, bleed, fart and secrete. We get spots, flakes and lumps and bumps. We cry, get scared, feel angry and sad at times. To try to hide all of this is impossible; being flawed is part of the deal. We cannot contort ourselves into neat little sweet-scented, smooth-skinned packages.

Anyhow, a perfect person would be pretty boring. Perfect people don't have anything to learn – and without learning, why are we here? We are here to be the brilliant, interesting and ever-evolving hot messes that we are.

The worst part of perfectionism is the self-judgement that often accompanies it. We believe that only when we're perfect are we worthwhile. Every time you inevitably fall short of perfection, you give yourself a hard time. Again, it's you who's judging you, then projecting that judgement on to others. The reality is that no one notices or cares about the tiny mistake in your email. The awkwardness of the question you ask at the dinner party isn't even noticed by anyone else, and saying no to drinks after work because you're exhausted doesn't make you a fun-spoiling loser, just a tired human.

If you think about it, appearing perfect in the eyes of every person you meet is impossible. You're trying to contort yourself to meet all their different and varied ideal standards. To appear perfect to everyone, you'd have to be a different person to each one! Oh, and if a person really is judging you for being imperfect, do you want them in your life anyway?

. . . .

Exercise: change your self-talk around perfectionism

We're often much more forgiving of others than we are of ourselves. When you get stuck in a perfectionist thought, try answering back with something more rational and positive by imagining what a friend would say to you. They might say something like this:

'Everyone says the wrong thing at times and it's really no big deal.'

'You are so much more than your appearance – imperfections are beautiful when you embrace them.'

'No one is perfect!'

'Your best is always enough.'

'Don't let perfect get in the way of great.'

'Everyone makes mistakes at times, it's just being human.'

'If someone is judging you harshly, it's usually the case they're judging themselves too.'

'Done is better than perfect.'

'If some people don't like you – that's all right. It's impossible to be liked by everyone.'

. . . .

Summary

★ Trying to be perfect is exhausting and stops us from being our true selves.

★ If you find yourself having perfectionist thoughts or feelings, imagine what you'd say to a friend in your position.

CHAPTER 11

Become your own judge

No one can make you
feel inferior without your consent
ELEANOR ROOSEVELT

Who are you to judge yourself? Do you somehow know better than your friends, family and partner who love and adore you? If your child is your number one fan, your best mate thinks you're the shit and your manager can't get enough of you, maybe it's time to believe them and put the evil self-judgement down to the ol' inner critic rather than reality.

A word about judgement

If you're feeling judged by someone else, remember this: judgemental people are often their own worst critics. Your dad, for whom nothing was ever good enough, your bitchy friend who points out your leg hair, or your sister who thinks you should stop being so picky and get married already are likely just as harsh on themselves as they are towards you, if not more so. As author Gabby Bernstein says, 'Judgement is a form of defence.' It's their ego's attempt to elevate itself by trampling on you. The same is true if you judge others. Your critical voice – the one that constantly puts other people down – will also find it impossible to ignore your own flaws.

The truth is, people who love and are secure in themselves

don't feel the need to judge, bitch or put others down. Oh, and for the person doing the judging, any boost in self-esteem from putting someone down will be short lived. What Buddha said about anger is true about judgemental thoughts, too: if you're holding hot coals with the intention of throwing them at someone else, you're the one who gets burned.

My inner mean girl

I used to get so triggered by women I believed were 'showing off'. I'd automatically think they were too confident: 'Who does she think she is?!' I'd mentally try to bring her down a peg or two by noticing all the ways she wasn't that great.

Then, I realized the reason I was triggered by unapologetic women was down to my own envy. I wished I could be that confident too. Having been raised to believe showing off was bad, I judged others because I was suppressing my own inner show-off! Some part of me also believed if I could lower this other woman to my level, I'd feel better about myself.

The more aware I became of this pattern, the more I noticed that 1) being judgey doesn't work as a self-esteem boosting strategy, and 2) I felt a bit yuck because the reality is, we are all in this together. As human beings, and especially as women, we have more similarities than differences, and we need to stick together and support one another.

Nobody wants to live in a judgemental world. But we've grown up in a culture where putting women down is the norm. In the media, women's bodies get picked apart, people openly post abuse about women who appear on reality TV, and we feel free to comment negatively on everything from Taylor Swift's relationship status to whether someone is a 'real' feminist or not because she wears high heels.

It's so easy to fall into the habit of talking badly about others. We do it to get things off our chest, let off steam, have a laugh or to bond with others. But as Buddha also said, it's a bit like drinking poison and expecting the other person to die. You're the one who is poisoned. It's also important to remember that the people you bitch to may well be saying the same about you.

The great news is, I believe this is a perfect example of where we can 'be the change we wish to see'. The same negative and critical part of you that bitches about your colleague behind her back is the part that puts yourself down too. How can we learn to love and accept ourselves if we're constantly criticizing our sisters? If we want to change the culture of one-up*woman*ship, it needs to start with us.

So if you don't have anything nice to say about someone, don't say anything at all. If you have an issue with someone, deal with them directly, don't go behind their back.

A few years ago, I made a decision that I don't want to be involved in gossip and bitchiness. I'm inviting you to join me. Imagine a world where women support each other and encourage each other to be our best selves. How much more successful and confident could we be?

. . . .

Exercise: be a bitch-free zone

If you want to love yourself more and accept yourself, learning to be less judgemental of others is an important stepping stone. Make a commitment to refrain from talking negatively about others behind their backs, remove yourself from bitchy conversations and let others know that you don't want to speak badly about people who aren't there.

. . . .

Summary

★ If someone is overly critical of you, they are most likely critical of themselves too.

★ Sometimes we judge others to try to boost our own self-esteem – but this doesn't work.

CHAPTER 12

The strength of setting boundaries

The concept of 'boundaries' has only recently crossed over from therapy speak to everyday conversation. So many of us still don't know what they are or why they're so important. Your boundaries are simply what is and what isn't OK with you. Examples might be: letting your sister know it's not OK with you that she only gets in touch when she needs a favour; or telling your colleague that when she repeatedly asks you questions it's hard for you to focus on your work.

Setting boundaries is being honest and open with people by letting them know what is and isn't OK with you. Psychotherapist and speaker Andrea Mathews has a great definition: 'Boundaries have to do with ownership. My ownership. My ownership of my own person, my own choices, my own power to speak, power to do, power to be.'[1]

Very few of us are taught about boundaries from an early age. As babies we're picked up and passed around by numerous strangers, made to hug and kiss Uncle Stu with the bad breath (when we don't want to), and told what to do by adults, with little explanation.

If you've never had your needs acknowledged, it can be hard to know what your needs actually are, let alone put them first and learn to tell people what they are too. But modern life is so demanding, creating your own healthy boundaries is, in fact, an essential act of self-care and emotional survival.

If you have no boundaries, people will walk all over you. Maybe what Gemma, aged thirty, describes sounds familiar?

If so, you likely need to work on your boundaries too. 'I always want to do what's best for other people and what suits them. I will work through lunch breaks just to fit in time to help colleagues. I will change plans to go along with friends. I also feel huge guilt if I say no to anyone, and that I have to make it up to them.'

At first, it might seem as though setting boundaries could threaten your relationships. But in fact, boundaries are essential for healthy relationships, both personal and professional, and will have a positive effect on them long term. For some relationships, setting boundaries will make it clear to you who doesn't have your best interests at heart, or who has been benefitting from your lack of boundaries. Once you've made it clear what is and isn't acceptable to you, it allows you to manage your energy, feel safe and be at your best. Setting boundaries also improves your confidence because it helps you feel empowered and in control.

My client Anna, forty-three, is a busy mum who works for a company with offices in the USA. She'd often find herself answering emails late into the night because the US office was five hours behind. Her boss had become used to her doing this. But these extra work hours were making it impossible for Anna to spend quality time with her children in the evenings. Through our work together, Anna came to realize she had set up the expectation that she'd always be available on email. She was dreading having the boundary-setting conversation with her boss, but when she told her that she'd no longer be available after 7 p.m., her boss respected this. Anna wished she'd felt able to have the conversation sooner.

That's not to say setting boundaries won't feel hard. You may be scared to bring up difficult topics in case the other person gets angry or upset. Or you may think if you don't keep doing what the other person wants, they won't love you any more. Henry Cloud and John Townsend, authors of *Boundaries: When To Say Yes, How to Say No, To Take Control of Your Life*, describe this dilemma perfectly:

> When we begin to set boundaries with people we love, a really hard thing happens: they hurt. They may feel a hole where you used to plug up their aloneness, their disorganization, or their financial irresponsibility. Whatever it is, they will feel a loss. If you love them, this will be difficult for you to watch. But, when you are dealing with someone who is hurting, remember your boundaries are both necessary for you and helpful for them. If you have been enabling them to be irresponsible, your limit setting may nudge them toward responsibility.

If you're being the caretaker of the other person's emotions or rescuing them, they'll never learn to handle them on their own. You may have to tell your sister you're not able to drop your life to look after her kids tonight, that you need more advance notice. Or say no to your friend who borrows clothes but doesn't give them back. Or tell your housemate you can't listen again to the whole story of her break-up, when it's the fifth time with the same boyfriend. Making the other person more responsible is ultimately empowering for them as well as for you.

You're the one who sets the precedent and creates the expectation. So you have to be the person responsible for creating your own boundaries. It will be scary. But no one else is going to do this for you. Only you have the power.

Other people's feelings are theirs

In order to feel braver when it comes to creating boundaries, it's good to remind ourselves we are not responsible for anyone else's feelings. Remember the last time you had a big birthday party and invited all your different groups of friends? And your night was somewhat ruined because you couldn't stop fretting if everyone was having a good time? This is you taking too much responsibility for other people's feelings.

Spoiler alert: you are not the customer satisfaction manager of the whole world. A friend recently told me, she felt responsible for the feelings of everyone she came into contact with. 'Phew, that is a lot of responsibility,' I told her. If you're experiencing that pressure on a near-constant basis, it's bloody exhausting.

I want to remind you, you cannot control how other people feel. The notion we can seems pretty ridiculous when you see it written in black and white – 'I can control how other people feel' – and even more so when you say it out loud (try it!). Everyone is living in their own universe, seeing it through their own special glasses, coloured by their experiences, beliefs, emotional baggage, education. This is what determines how someone feels, not you. Your job is simply to get to know yourself while being mindful of other people's feedback and then . . . let go. Next time you're putting pressure on yourself to keep everyone happy, remind yourself of this.

· ·

Exercise: **lessons from the future you**

Imagine two chairs in front of you. In the left-hand chair, see yourself one year in the future, not having changed anything about the way you behave, your relationships, your boundaries. What do you notice about her? What does she say? How does she feel? What is she doing with her life?
Now imagine a second future you on the right-hand chair. This is a you who has made significant progress at being more

assertive, brave and confident. She has set her boundaries. What do you notice about this future you? What does she say? How does she feel? What is she doing with her life? What advice does she have for you about how to get to where she is now?

. . . .

Listening to yourself and what your needs are

At a recent workshop I attended, we did an exercise designed to tune us into what we find comfortable in terms of personal space, and our physical boundaries. We were paired up with a stranger, and asked to use hand movements to signal to the other person to move closer or further away. We were instructed to notice how we felt with the other person at different distances. When my partner got very close, less than a foot away, I began to feel a distinct discomfort in my chest. As I signalled for her to move further away, the feeling went away.

Tuning in to how you feel is not only useful for physical boundaries, but for all boundaries. Ask yourself: how does this make me feel? If someone makes you uncomfortable, it's a clue they have crossed a line.

During this exercise, I also noticed how guilty I felt when asking the other person to move away from me. Even in this incredibly safe environment, I realized I was wondering whether she felt rejected by me. It gave me a massive insight: that we're not always conscious just how often we put the feelings and opinions of other people before our own. It happens on autopilot. Perhaps you've held off handing in your notice because you don't want to let down your team, or had sex sooner than you wanted to keep someone happy, or stayed friends with someone you disliked so as not to hurt their feelings. As women, we tend to put our feelings and needs second all the time.

Setting boundaries creates a virtuous circle of self-esteem. If you're letting people walk all over you, it could be because you don't feel you're worth sticking up for. People may start to take advantage because you're sending the message that you don't respect yourself and will go along with anything. The fastest way to change a belief is to take action. Setting boundaries is a powerful message to yourself and to others about your worth and value. Firmly standing up for what's right for you will give you confidence. Taking action will change the way others respond to you, which will, in turn, make setting boundaries easier.

. . . .

Exercise: what are my boundaries?

Your boundaries are based on your needs. Go through each of these categories, working out your needs and setting a boundary for each one.

Phone boundaries. When you're available to answer calls, reply to texts and interact on social media.

Sleep boundaries. The time you go to bed and wake up.

Email boundaries. When you are available and willing to reply to emails.

Physical boundaries. Your personal space, when and where you're happy to be touched.

Sexual boundaries. What is and isn't OK with you sexually.

Emotional boundaries. Separating your feelings from the feelings of someone else. Not taking on the burden of, or responsibility for, other people's feelings.

Financial boundaries. When you're happy to lend money, or pay, and when you're not.

Time with others. How much time you spend with family, friends and children, how much time you need for yourself. How much time you're happy to spend doing favours and helping out.

. . . .

Advice for communicating your boundaries

- Make eye contact and be aware of your body language. Sit or stand confidently, shoulders back, with an open posture and your head high.
- Talk from your perspective without blaming the other person. Use statements that begin with 'I' – I need, I want, I think, I feel.
- State what you want and need clearly. Be direct and don't expect the other person to read your mind.

Here are some examples of what you might say.

To your child who you'd like to be more responsible: 'From now on, I'd like you to pack your own school bag/clear the table/keep your room tidy. I'll be available to help you – just ask – but I won't do it for you.'

To the friend who only gets in touch and asks to see you at the last minute: 'I'd love to see you tonight, but in future I'd like to know a couple of weeks beforehand because it's hard for me to arrange my other commitments at short notice.'

To your intern who has come to rely on you too much to check their work: 'I am still happy to look over your work when you've done it. But I know you're capable, so from now on I'd like you to get it to the stage where you consider it finished before you show it to me.'

Summary

★ Setting boundaries is about letting others know what is and isn't OK with you.

★ Boundaries can improve relationships because they bolster your self-worth and value.

★ You set a precedent for how others treat you; when you set boundaries, people start to treat you better.

CHAPTER 13

How to please yourself

Girls are more likely to be sticklers when it comes to rules, to be obeyers of authority and keepers of the peace. We're socialized to be aware of other people's feelings. And if you were, at an early age, given a doll that does 'real' wees and needs to have its nappy changed, you'll have experience of being taught to take care of others. Do you recognize there's a rule-following, nice-playing, thinking-of-others good girl inside you?

As a child and in my early teens, I felt so much pressure to be a good girl. In my view, I was responsible for my parents' feelings. I tried to keep them happy by making sure my room was always spotless, emptying the dishwasher and folding my clothes and putting them away in my drawer, being well behaved and going to bed early. That's not to say I was always well behaved. As you know, I could throw a tantrum in a supermarket as fiendishly as the next child. But I remember often being inhibited by my need to play by the rules. When my teenage friends started drinking in the park, for example, I was so terrified of being caught and told off, I stuck to Diet Cokes while my friends chugged cheap cider.

When I was aged twelve, my dad, wondering why I wasn't home in time for my curfew, popped his head around the door of my best friend's thirteenth birthday party. The film *The Full Monty* had recently been released on VHS and the boys at the party, inspired by the Chippendale antics of the lead characters, were conducting a striptease, much to the girls' amusement. It was all fairly innocent, but my dad, faced with four topless twelve-year-old boys and fearing I was involved in a pre-teen orgy, shut down the party and dragged me home. I was mortified, and my fear of being caught misbehaving was cemented.

Until my late twenties, my good girl senses stayed on high alert, keeping watch for any rules that I might inadvertently break or any expressions of offence about my actions.

Good girl behaviours are reinforced in childhood by parents and teachers. That's because good girls are no trouble. We behave in class, we do our homework and empty the dishwasher without being asked. We're conditioned by praise and encouragement to keep behaving in this way. But when the patterns formed in childhood continue into adulthood, they can be challenging to deprogramme.

Rachel Simmons, author of *The Curse of the Good Girl*, talks about the pressure to be nice all the time, to be friends with everyone, to be liked at all costs, to be pleasing, passive and perfect. How from a young age we experience pressure to be skinny, perfect girls who never put a foot wrong, upset anyone or make mistakes. Put like that, doesn't it sound exhausting?

Even now I'm an adult, the difference between my worldview and my boyfriend's is palpable. His attitude to rules goes like this: 'Do what you want until someone tells you not to (as long as it doesn't hurt anyone else).' Meanwhile, I'm the one taking the rules too far. Two recent examples: 'Is it really OK to sit in that section of the restaurant if we're just having drinks?' And, 'Should we be taking our own popcorn into the cinema as it's not allowed . . . and we might get caught!'

If something goes wrong, I blame myself, while he blames the other person or puts it down to bad luck. I take things personally, while his familiar refrain is, 'They're the one with the problem.' He's able to let things go, while I mull them over for hours. Does he apologize for his crazy morning hair and baggy, food-stained activewear? Hell, no. I'll admit some of this is down to personality, but we appear to be following a typical gender-based pattern.

You might be asking, what's the problem here? It's nice to be nice, right? But issues arise when we can't stick up for ourselves, speak our minds or ask for what we need. And when we can't bring ourselves to bend or break arbitrary, unwritten rules that desperately need it, like pleasing everyone and being undemanding. If we're so used to putting the needs of others first, how can we learn to get our own basic needs met? Or if we're so afraid of others thinking we're bossy, how can we ask for a raise or make ourselves heard in a meeting? Good girls, sadly, finish last.

I don't believe the answer is acting like a man or being a bitch to get what you want. The answer is, not being afraid of being disliked in the pursuit of what's right for you. It's about reclaiming your prerogative to go for opportunities, asking for what you need and putting yourself first instead of last. It's about being who you are without fear.

Are you a people pleaser?

I can't give you a sure-fire formula for success, but I can give you a formula for failure: try to please everybody all the time.

HERBERT BAYARD

Even Beyoncé has confessed to suffering from this. She told *Elle* magazine: 'I'm a people pleaser, I hold a lot of things in. I'm always making sure everybody is okay.' In a world where Queen B struggles with this, there must be something wrong. But what happens when we, like Bey, hold things in?

Sarah, twenty-five, told me, 'I always think about what other people would expect or like. I will sacrifice the things I want to do for the good of someone else. I don't have the assertiveness to say "I would like to do this" if it will upset someone else. I'm a nurturing person but my behaviour has now gone way beyond that. I seem to spend a lot of my personal and professional time making others' problems go away while ignoring my own until they explode!'

Chances are, your habit of people pleasing came from your childhood or early life experience. If you were rewarded for being 'Mummy's little helper' you'll have been conditioned to believe being helpful is good and worthwhile. If, growing up, being a good listener and a selfless friend to others earned you popularity or respect, those behaviours were reinforced. As children we take the reactions and feelings of people around us to be a result of something we have done. And so we learn to derive our self-esteem from being the caring one who puts others first or is always helping others. You might even have grown up in an environment where pleasing others was the only way to feel safe, and now it's an ingrained habit.

Don't get me wrong, I'm not saying it's wrong to help others. Far from it. But there is a dark side to people pleasing. It's when being a helpful friend turns into martyrdom. Or if you're burning out because you've exhausted yourself by not meeting your own needs. Or, deep down, you're secretly seething with rage at being taken advantage of. These are all signs your desire to help others has gone too far.

The truth is, if we base our self-worth on the approval of others, we'll always be on shaky ground. And if we expect other people to give us our self-esteem, we're giving away our power.

The teacher and author Byron Katie sums it up brilliantly in her audiobook *Your Inner Awakening*: 'It's the biggest fallacy that "I can manipulate you to love me". We're living our lives as a facade, and we can't feel approved of until we approve of ourselves.'

As much as we'd all like to believe doing things to please others has a positive effect on them, I'd argue that it does the opposite. If pleasing is coming from a place of desperation and resentment or even manipulation (usually unconscious) you're really not doing the other person any favours. Because suppressing yourself and putting on a mask of agreeableness while inside you're a suffering, angry, exhausted mess is not authentic.

I don't know about you but, for me, learning this was a bitter pill to swallow. What do you mean, being a people pleaser is actually selfish?! If being 'too nice' has become a part of your identity, as it had for me, becoming true to yourself feels daunting. You can start by taking more responsibility for your relationship with yourself – that means being kind to yourself – as well as realizing you are not responsible for the thoughts and feelings of others.

Growing and changing is uncomfortable. As you start to put yourself first, you will undeniably challenge people's perceptions of you. You will begin to create a new way of being, and others might not love it at first. But remember: you'll be paving the way not only for more integrity for yourself but also for more authentic and positive relationships with others too.

. . . .

Exercise: what do I really think or feel?

Asking yourself these questions will tune you into what you really think and feel. Get into the habit of asking yourself:

What do I want?

If nobody else's opinion matters, what would I choose?

What decision is most in line with my purpose, values, beliefs or passions?

What does my intuition tell me is the right answer?

What would I do if I was putting myself first?

Summary

★ If you were praised for being a good girl as a child, you may be a people pleaser now.

★ When we put everyone before ourselves, we can end up burning out or getting resentful.

★ Get into the habit of asking yourself: 'What do I really think, feel or want?'

CHAPTER 14

Discover the power of 'no'

When you say yes to something you don't want to do,
here is the result: you hate what you are doing,
you resent the person who asked you, and
you hurt yourself.

JAMES ALTUCHER, *THE POWER OF NO*

One of the shortest words in the English language is also the hardest to say. It's easy to say yes (even though we might regret it later). Saying no can be tough even for the sturdiest among us.

The essential reason we struggle to say no is, we're worried what people will think. Psychologist Dr Vanessa Bohns, Associate Professor of Organizational Behavior at Cornell University says, 'Saying no feels threatening to our relationships.' Will they judge us? Will they then reject us? Will we hurt their feelings and make them feel rejected? Will they get angry? Will we damage our relationship or lose them as a friend?

What you have to remember is, saying no is good for your mental, physical, emotional and financial health. It's a powerful act of self-care and self-love.

If you frequently regret saying yes – to cooking dinner when you're exhausted, or helping a colleague with their work as a favour although you're at capacity – you're likely a conscientious person who keeps your word when you commit to something, even at risk to your own peace of mind or well-being. You might be used to putting the needs of others before yourself. Or maybe it's that you're insecure and saying yes to everything is your way of keeping others happy so they don't 'abandon' you.

There have been numerous times in the past when I've said yes to an invitation because it felt too awkward to decline, only to go but resent every minute because I wanted to be elsewhere. Or worse, times when I've cancelled at the last minute because I didn't have time, felt under pressure or simply hadn't dared to refuse in the first place.

We martyr ourselves for the feelings of other people. Do you really think your boss doesn't know you secretly hate having to work late when you're knackered? Resentment seeps out of you like bin juice and other people can sense your martyrdom, if only unconsciously. Even if you keep it well hidden, it's only a matter of time before you burn out, have a meltdown or explode with anger.

· ·

Exercise: **lost time meditation**

Teacher and speaker Araminta Barbour taught me this meditation. It's designed to inspire you to find and stick to your 'no'.

> Close your eyes, take some deep breaths and relax. Let your mind drift back, to reflect on all the time, energy and money you've wasted saying yes to things you didn't really want to do. All the films you didn't want to watch, the coffees you had with people you didn't want to have them with, the meetings you sat through you didn't need to attend, the weddings you couldn't afford to be at.

Reflect on all the minutes and hours, energy and cold hard cash you'll never get back. Allow yourself to feel a little angry.

Channel the energy of your anger into deciding to set firmer boundaries and finding your 'no' more easily.

. . . .

Say no to say yes

Perhaps you're lucky enough to have numerous opportunities and requests come your way so it's hard to know what to say yes to and what to decline? You might be invited to start a business with a friend, complete a cycling challenge, go to a music festival or for after-work drinks. Even though each one seems tempting and you can't think of a good reason to say no, they could still be a massive drain on your time, money and energy. (Anyone who's spent hundreds of pounds at a festival and three days recovering afterwards would agree!)

Derek Sivers, entrepreneur and founder of CD Baby, shares a simple way to make your decision easier. If something isn't a 'hell yeah!', it's a 'no'. Derek writes: 'When you say no to most things, you leave room in your life to really throw yourself completely into that rare thing that makes you say, "HELL YEAH!"'

You can apply this test to almost every area of your life, from work to friendships to whether or not you should go to bed with the person you just started dating. If it's not a 'hell yeah, honey' it's gotta be a 'no'.

At first, it might be hard to say no because people are used to being able to call on you, their yes gal. Over many years you've set a precedent of being someone who's always available, happy to help, take on more work, bake the cake or join the party. It's incredible you're now breaking free of this old pattern that has held you back. Even acknowledging you're doing this is an act of courage. You're doing amazingly, so let's keep going!

I say no so I can say yes

You can do anything, but not everything.
DAVID ALLEN, *GETTING THINGS DONE*

For me, writing this book has been an excellent lesson in the power of no. I've had to turn down interviews, speaking gigs, events and offers of coffee or lunch, not because they wouldn't be lovely to do, but because I need to create the time for my top priority right now, this book.

Saying no can seem negative, but here's the thing: it's actually one of the most positive things to do. We only have so much time and energy each day. Are you going to spend it on what really matters to you? Or are you going to waste it because you're worried what someone might think of you? When you say no to someone else, you are saying yes to yourself and what's really important to you. So, each time you have a choice, ask yourself: 'If I say no, what am I saying yes to?'

- I'm saying yes to a bath and an early night on Friday so I can feel amazing on Saturday.
- I'm saying yes to having the weekend to myself.
- I'm saying yes to quality time with my family.
- I'm saying yes to having a hangover-free Monday.
- I'm saying yes to finishing this passion project.
- I'm saying yes to my mental health and well-being.

Author and entrepreneur Stephen Covey shares a story about how we can make sure that our highest priorities (our hell yeahs) are taken care of. He tells the story of getting a large, wide-mouthed mason jar and filling it with fist-sized rocks. He then asks, is the jar full? Most people say yes. Next, he pours in some gravel, then some smaller stones fill in the gaps between the larger stones. He asks, is the jar full now? Then he pours in some sand. And finally, some water. What his story illustrates is: if we don't put in our big rocks – our priorities, our hell yeahs – first, there's no way they'll fit in after we've put in the small rocks, the sand, the water – all the things everyone else wants us to do.

. . . .

Exercise: schedule your hell yeahs

What things are a hell yeah to you? What are the most import-ant to your well-being and happiness? How would you most like to spend your time?

Schedule your number one priorities into your diary . . . then watch how everything else fits in around them.

. . . .

How to face your worst-case scenario

If you say no, what's the worst that could happen? You may think something along these lines:

- I'll be abandoned because my partner will no longer see me as amenable and easy-going.
- My friend who's come to rely on me will be hurt, and she'll ditch me.
- My boss will fire me because I'm no longer 'a team player'.

- My child wanted desperately to go to the funfair so if I say no, I'll be wracked with guilt about putting her through the pain of disappointment.
- The person I say no to will get angry, which makes saying no feel unsafe.

Ask yourself: is your worst case really true?

Have you tested it? What actually happens when you start to let people know what is and isn't OK with you? Much of the time, you'll find you're thinking the worst when the reality is, you can manage whatever the consequences turn out to be. Often, the people who matter won't mind, and in fact, people will respect you and your boundaries as a result.

If I say no, am I going to miss out?

By saying yes to everything, what are you really missing out on? Feeling rested and energetic? Having more time for yourself? Feeling free and empowered by your own decisions? Own your choices and remind yourself of all you're saying yes to.

What is the cost of saying yes to this?

When growing a business or pushing ahead in your career, you might find yourself swimming in opportunities to prove yourself and overrun with chances to meet new and exciting people. This chance might never come again, right? You need to strike while the iron is hot, knuckle down and say goodbye to nights in on the sofa and washing your hair, for the next year at least!

It's easy to get into a scarcity mindset and feel as though we have to hoover up opportunities as they arise. But what is the real cost? Many of us chase success at the expense of our well-being and some people continue on this treadmill of over-working for their whole careers. According to Bronnie Ware, author of *The Top Five Regrets of the Dying*, 'I wish I hadn't worked so hard' is number two on the list of people's biggest deathbed regrets. (Number one, by the way, is 'I wish I'd had the courage to live a life true to myself, not the life others expected of me', which couldn't be more relevant to what we're tackling in this book.)

Saying no is an essential aspect of becoming more successful in your career. As Warren Buffett, one of the most affluent inves-tors of all time, famously said, 'The difference between success-ful people and really successful people is that really successful people say no to almost everything.' If taking your success in business or your personal life to the next level is important to you, getting better at saying no is a vital part of the equation.

. . . .

Exercise: what to say no to

Make a list. You'll probably want to include some of these examples as well as your own.

Meetings you know, deep down, don't require you to be there.

Relationships that drain you or drag you down.

Anything you strongly resent doing.

Anything that puts your mental well-being at risk.

Any romantic or sexual advances that make you feel uncomfortable.

. . . .

Five keys to saying no

1. Be kind

If you can say no kindly and politely, you can still leave the person feeling good about their interaction with you. Compliment and congratulate them! Let them know you're sure it will be an incredible event and you'll be sad to miss it, or praise the success of the project you can't help them with. When you're coming from an empowered place of owning your 'no', it's easier to keep your cool and remain calm and this, in turn, will allow you to be as kind as you can while saying no.

2. Be honest

It's OK to say you're busy – even if you're just busy having a bath and an early night – but don't make up a fake excuse. Especially when it comes to friends and loved ones. They will appreciate honesty. If you're not being authentic, they'll smell it a mile off. Lies will only come back to bite you.

3. Let them know it's not personal

Author and entrepreneur Tim Ferriss suggested this strategy on a podcast episode about saying no.[1] Letting them know you're on a 'no meeting diet' for the next four months or that you have a 'policy' of not going out on weeknights will allow you to state your needs while ensuring the other person doesn't think it's about them.

4. Offer an alternative

Maybe you can't help someone out this week, but you have more free time next month so you can offer them that instead? If you can't help someone in the way they've asked, is there another way you can support them?

5. Be consistent

If you fold and end up saying yes after an initial no, people will come to see you as a someone who isn't true to their word, or who can be persuaded. Being consistent and holding your boundaries is vital for your integrity and setting the expectation that you mean what you say.

Don't fall into the trap of over-explaining

Never explain - your friends do not need it and your
enemies will not believe you anyway.
ELBERT HUBBARD

Obviously, there are some situations when an explanation is necessary. Telling a friend you can't go to her wedding because you've already agreed to go to someone else's is important because it will help her understand why. But other times, we over-explain to try to control the other person's perception of us, or because we're put on the spot, flustered or wriggling to get out of the obligation. Lying and making up a convoluted story that may well backfire is not cool or OK. It's true, we often do this because we're trying to maintain the connection and that person's opinion of us. But it can also go wrong if our explanation seems to them like the beginning of a negotiation . . . then we end up caving in and saying yes.

For example, over-explaining by saying 'I'm sorry, I can't come out tonight because I said I'd make dinner for my house-mate' opens the door for the other person to persuade you. 'Can't you just come for one drink then cook afterwards?' At this point, your resolve for saying no may be depleted and you find yourself going out for one – or more – drinks when what you really needed was a quiet night in.

Worse still, over-explaining can seem phoney. Research shows people who are lying give a lot of extra, superfluous information but those telling the truth often use less detail. So keep your explanation short and to the point.

Saying no without offering a lengthy explanation also sends others a message of confidence. 'No' can be a complete sentence. If you genuinely have an excuse, the people who love you likely won't need to hear it, and those who aren't your biggest fans probably won't believe you anyway!

Here are some scripts and language for you to use:

- 'I wish I could but . . .'
- 'I'm fully booked for new projects right now.'
- 'I've got a policy of not taking on any more work until July, until this busy period is over.'
- 'Your event looks amazing – but I'm afraid I've got too much on my plate to be involved right now.'
- 'I'd love to help but at the moment I can't.'
- 'It would be great to catch up – but I can't this week.'

When you're caught off guard

If the request is unexpected, you can easily find yourself agreeing to something you don't want to do. Put on the spot, it's hard to think clearly. But you can always be prepared with phrases that buy you time until you can think. These are also useful if it feels too awkward to say no right away. You can give a solid 'no' later on.

Here are some phrases to use:

- 'Let me get back to you on that.'
- 'I'll check my diary and let you know.'
- 'Give me a few days to think about it.'

Saying no to friends and loved ones

These are usually the hardest people of all to say no to, especially when you're being asked to help someone who needs it. As women, we're socialized from a young age to put the needs of others before ourselves so it can feel almost unnatural to put yourself first.

Of course, there are times when you'll choose to say yes, to the things that really matter. I personally hate helping people to move house – I mean, how am I supposed to know where all the boxes go?! But am I going to help my sister pack up her stuff and haul it across town if she needs me? Of course I am.

However, before you say yes, I think it's important to ask yourself these questions:

- 'Am I sacrificing my own mental or physical health for this?'
- 'Am I going to resent having to do this?'
- 'How would the other person feel if they knew I really didn't want to be there?'

Most of us would be horrified if we knew someone we loved was only saying yes to please us. Or worse, saying yes was seriously inconvenient or even a threat to their mental health. We'd much prefer the other person to be honest, wouldn't we?

In her TED Talk 'Good Boundaries Free You', family therapist and author Sarri Gilman discusses how we all have an inner compass which lets us know if something is a yes or a no for us. But she continues: 'Sometimes that compass gets clouded, and this can happen when we've been ignoring our compass or arguing with it because we don't like what it's saying.' So, if we've got used to putting others first, it can be hard to know what it is that we want any more. To sum up, she says: 'You can't let the emotions of another person determine your boundaries.'

Setting boundaries can be stressful. It may make you perspire, cringe and curl your toes when you first start to set them but, as I talked about before, it's a long-term strategy to living a calmer, happier life.

Being on the receiving end of a loved one's anger, hurt or outrage can be incredibly uncomfortable. The temptation to change your mind or rush in and try to fix it may be substantial. If they're used to you saying yes all the time, it might also be a shock for them to know they can't always rely on you (or exploit you).

You might find it helpful to practise beforehand what you'll say. And imagine staying strong and consistent, and explaining your reason for saying no without over-explaining. Can you imagine yourself feeling strong and assertive in the face of your loved one's anger?

Overcoming the guilt of saying no

Guilt is a pretty useless emotion. It's only helpful if it makes you change what you're doing when you know you've done wrong. What often happens is, we feel guilty due to the judgement of other people, not because we're unhappy with our choice.

The sad truth is, the only people who will get mad about you setting firmer boundaries are those who benefitted from you having none. Should you really feel guilty for putting things right?

Part of being brave is learning to tolerate the emotions of others and hold true to your integrity. To stay firm in your convictions, when things get intense. Doing all of this is like strengthening a muscle; you might feel weak at first, but with consistent flexing, it will get easier.

You may be experiencing guilt over important issues: that you can't be there more for your sick parent, or call your great-aunt more often. It's hard to come across a mother who doesn't experience mum guilt to some extent. Coming back to what is right for you, affirming to yourself and others why you're saying no, then owning your decision can make it less painful. Remember that there is only one of you, you're not perfect, and some situations are just tricky. Don't beat yourself up.

At the more extreme end of people pleasing is what psychologists call 'compassion fatigue', when people spend so much time caring for others, they don't look after themselves and so are at risk of burning out. You may have this to a lesser extent; you tend to put others' well-being before your own. In fact, when you're caring for someone else, you need to up your own self-care. You might also need to be extra vigilant about saying no and stricter about making time for yourself.

Think about it the other way; would you want your sister to babysit if you knew she was feeling overwhelmed and stretched to the max? Would you want your colleague to come out for drinks if she didn't want to be there? No! So why should it be any different for you? It's unlikely people are going to think you're a terrible friend, daughter or employee, just because you had to put yourself first and say no. Most of us judge ourselves more harshly than other people do. How would you feel if someone said no to you for a similar reason to yours? What advice would you have for a friend in the same situation? Chances are, it wouldn't be the end of the world.

When you take care of yourself, you will have more to give to other people. You'll be in a better mood; you won't feel resentful for being forced to do something you didn't want to. You may find it makes your relationship better in the long run, even if it feels uncomfortable at first.

Saying no to your boss

Melissa, twenty-seven, told me, 'I needed to be honest about how I felt. I needed to realize that when I was stressed, my body was telling me something – and the stress was making me ill. So I said no to my boss when he tried to make me take on a project like the last one that made me ill. And I felt really proud of myself. I have learned to notice when I'm over-extended and to make sure I take a step back.'

Phrases to use:

- 'I've been prioritizing project X and I won't be able to take on board anything else at the moment. I could take this on if I put project X on hold.'
- 'I'm really busy today/this week/this month – who else could take on this work?'

Saying no to a friend

Phrases to use:

- 'Sorry, but I have a policy of not lending money to friends.'
- 'I'd love to help but I'm completely overstretched this week.'
- 'I'm so honoured you asked me to come to your wedding and although I'd love to join you on your special day, I just can't make it work financially at the moment.'

Saying no to a family member

Phrases to use:

- 'I loved spending Christmas with you last year, but we've decided to have a quiet one this year and spend it at home.'
- 'I want to help out but I've already made plans for that evening and I can't change them.'

Saying no to someone who wants free advice or to pick your brain

I get dozens of questions each week from people asking for help with their anxiety, or for business advice. And while it's lovely to be able to help others, if people are always asking for free help it can be a massive drain on energy and time. This is especially true when the advice someone is seeking is what you do for a job, and you can't afford to do for free what you usually get paid for.

Phrases to use:

- 'Thanks so much for getting in touch. While I'm not able to meet for coffee at the moment, you can book a consultation with me on my website. My fees start at £xyz an hour.'
- 'My diary is full at the moment but I wrote a blog post/book/have a product that solves this problem, and you can find it here.'

Saying no to someone you're not romantically interested in

Anyone who's ever been at the receiving end of a ghosting knows it's not cool. So instead of floating off into nothingness without a word, it's better to be honest and direct about how you're feeling.

Give an honest reason, such as:

- 'I don't feel there's chemistry between us.'
- 'I don't think our personalities are compatible.'

Saying no to someone crossing a line

Unfortunately, unwanted advances are, for women, pretty common. If, for example, your manager at work says something inappropriate, you could say, 'You're making me feel uncomfortable.' This is a good way to let them know how you feel and that what they said isn't OK.

You might have been accosted in the street by someone who starts asking you lots of questions in an attempt to engage you in conversation and hook you in. You might feel it's rude to cut them down, but if you're not interested, say so. Keep it short and polite. 'No, thanks!' Or, 'Thanks, but I'm not interested.'

Perhaps you've been known to say, 'I've got a boyfriend,' as a rebuff. If this isn't the truth, it's better to give an honest reason. They might see an excuse as an opening for negotiation, or treat it as an invitation to try to win your affection from said boyfriend.

However, there is an exception: when safety is an issue. Just yesterday, I saw a woman out running whose path was blocked by a group of men shouting, 'Alright, darling?' While this particular situation didn't come across as particularly threatening, it could have been. You might be concerned your 'no' will lead to the other person getting angry. If the interaction is making you uneasy, it's best to get away as quickly as possible.

If you think you've been at the receiving end of abuse, it's important to report it. Taking action could stop it from happening to someone else.

This example was in an article for the *Guardian* by Laura Bates of the Everyday Sexism Project. 'While out running on a reasonably busy street in broad daylight, I was stopped and asked for directions . . . I obliged and as I showed him on the map on my phone he looked down my top, made a sleazy remark then grabbed my breast . . . I calmly took his registration and went straight to the police. I was surprised by how seriously they took it. They thanked me for coming in! They agreed with me: this guy was out of order and his behaviour was not OK! He's been charged.'[2]

Saying no to sex

You might believe that because you've kissed someone or gone home with them, you're obliged or under pressure to have sex.

You aren't. Just because you said yes to or had sex with them before, it doesn't mean you have to say yes now. You have the right to change your mind.

From the women I've spoken to, it seems much of our fear of saying no to sex comes down to a fear of being rejected.

Sorrel, twenty, told me: 'I'd got myself into thinking this guy was the only one who would ever show interest in me, so who was I to say no? I was worried if I did I would be rejected, abandoned or replaced. To quell my deep-seated fear that I'd end up alone, I'd say yes to sex. After I started to say no more, I finally learned that saying no actually gains you more respect because you're being assertive. It doesn't make you selfish to say no to something you don't want to do.'

You don't owe your body to anyone. And if someone cares about you, they would not want you to feel uncomfortable about saying yes to sex. Plus if you're lying there, wishing it was over, it's hardly a recipe for sizzling sex for the other person! You deserve to be with someone who wants you to enjoy the experience as much as them.

It swings both ways. If you're using sex to manipulate the other person, that's not right either. Sure, there might be times when you're a bit tired for sex with your partner but you go along with it anyway. But feeling disgusted with yourself afterwards because you've gone against your own values is different.

As much as we'd like them to be, our partners are not mind-readers, and we need to get braver at saying no to what we don't want as well as asking for what we do.

Tune in to that inner compass and ask yourself, 'Is this a yes or a no for me?' 'Is this making me uncomfortable?' Read on for more about listening to yourself and what your needs are.

. . . .

Exercise: **list your no's**

Make a list of the things you want to say no to.
Then make a list of *exactly* what you will say.

. . . .

Exercise: **practise saying no**

Finding small ways to say no builds your 'no' muscle and gives you the confidence to say no in more serious or important moments. Where can you practise saying no today? Try declining the offer of more water from the waiter; saying, 'Not today, thanks!' to the chugger who tries to stop you in the street; or telling your colleague you can't come into the last-minute meeting.

. . . .

Own your choices

If you do say yes, own your decision. Remind yourself you're choosing to do it. The reality is, you don't have to do anything. You don't have to go to work; you choose to, so you can pay your bills. Even if you're stuck in a job that is far from ideal, you made a choice at some time to do it to support yourself or your family.

Everything is a choice, and it's empowering to remember that options are always available. Affirm, 'I am choosing to do this.'

Summary

★ Every time you say no to what isn't your top priority, you say yes to what is.

★ If it isn't a 'hell, yeah!' it should be a 'no'.

★ When you're put on the spot, saying 'Let me get back to you about that' can buy you time to formulate your no.

CHAPTER 15

Stop apologizing

Are you suffering from 'sorry syndrome'?

A few years ago I was in the supermarket with my boyfriend. As I browsed the frozen food aisle, someone backed into me and stood on my foot. I immediately exclaimed, 'Oh, I'm so sorry! Sorry!' Even though it clearly wasn't my fault. Later that evening, my boyfriend asked me, 'When are you going to stop apologizing for your very existence?' Apparently, apologizing had become a habit I hadn't even been aware of.

Here are some apologies I have made (and I know I'm not the only one!):

- 'Sorry about the mess.'
- 'Sorry, I'm not wearing any make-up, I look a state!'
- 'Sorry, but could I just ask a question?'
- 'Sorry, but this food is cold.'
- 'Sorry, can I sit here?'
- 'Sorry that you have to look at me in a bikini!'
- 'Sorry to bother you, but would you like a cup of tea?'

Well I, for one, am sick of this bullshit.

All these examples seem utterly ridiculous and unnecessary when we take a moment to reflect on them. But often, we are on autopilot. Apologies pour out of us before we've even had a chance to assess the situation.

But why DO we apologize so much? In my case, it was a sense of shame, a fear of disapproval and confrontation that led me to overuse the 'S' word. I didn't feel good enough, so I automatically assumed others were right and I was wrong.

There's also an apparent social advantage to apologizing; to keep the peace and avoid fights or confrontations. We might pre-empt a request with a 'sorry' so we don't come across as bossy or pushy. Or it can stem from imposter syndrome: we ask ourselves, 'Who am I to question a senior colleague?'

Of course, apologies do have a place; when we've done something wrong or made a mistake. And when we save our sorries for when they're genuinely appropriate, they'll carry more weight and authenticity.

You are worthy; you have a right to be here, you have a right to take up space, to speak up, and to be seen and heard. You're not a bitch for asking for what you want, and you look just great without make-up. You don't owe a made-up face to anyone!

It might seem as if sorry is 'just a word', but the language we use to speak to ourselves and others is important. The words we choose create images, thoughts and feelings in our minds and the minds of others. They send a message and create meaning for us. When we over-apologize, we take the blame for something that isn't our fault and, as we do that, it saps our confidence.

An unnecessary sorry puts us below the other person. We create a feeling we're somehow 'less than' – not worthy, or deficient. It hurts our credibility and puts us in a subservient position. We give our power away. It can impact our position in the workplace, our relationships and stop us from getting what we want (like warm food in a restaurant, a raise at work, or more help around the house).

One powerful technique I'd suggest, is to swap sorry for another word.

Thank you

Instead of saying, 'I'm sorry you had to come with me to the doctor's appointment,' say, 'Thank you for coming with me.' Another example might be to say, 'Thank you for waiting for me,' or, 'Thanks for listening to me.' Feelings of gratitude are way more productive and feel-good than those of apology. Saying thanks will pump the other person full of positive vibes too.

Excuse me

Would 'excuse me' be a more appropriate phrase to use in its place? 'Excuse me, my food is cold, could you get me a replacement please?' Or, 'Excuse me, I'd like to get past.' Or, 'Excuse me, I've been waiting in this queue for half an hour.'

Please

Or perhaps please fits better. Asking a question doesn't require an apology. 'Could you please clarify what you mean?' Or, 'Could you please say that again?' Or, 'Please could you do the washing up?'

. . . .

Exercise: when do you apologize unnecessarily?
When is your 'sorry' not real?

Think of five situations where you over-apologize and make a note of them:

1. . . . .

2. . . . .

3. . . . .

4. . . . .

5. . . . .

Think of what you could say instead – try 'excuse me', 'thank you' and 'please'. Or could you lose the 'sorry' completely, replace it with nothing?

Summary

★ Many of us say sorry far more often than is necessary, and this can impact our confidence.

★ Think about what you could say instead of the word 'sorry' – are 'excuse me' or 'please' more relevant?

PART FOUR

How to fail yourself better

CHAPTER 16

Freeing yourself from fear of failure

*Think like a queen. A queen is not afraid to fail. Failure
is another stepping stone to greatness.*
OPRAH WINFREY

Fear of failure can be paralysing. You've heard of the fight-
or-flight response to fear – but did you know there's also a
'freeze' response? It's when we get stuck in inaction and procrastination.

We know that if we don't try, we'll fail by default. But still,
a lack of confidence and self-esteem holds us back from going
for the jobs, relationships or friendships we want, from starting businesses or attempting new hobbies. For some, it's about
what people will think if we are seen to try and fail. For others,
it's what people will think of us if we succeed. While failure
is a frightening prospect, success can sometimes seem even
scarier.

As women, we seem to struggle with criticism more than
men. As we discussed before, from a young age we're socialized to care what others think, to keep the peace, to please
others, to do things correctly. We're more likely to get
wrapped up in cotton wool and be overprotected by our
parents. I wrote about this phenomenon, 'the skinned knee
effect', in *The Anxiety Solution*. Boys are encouraged to play
rough, get muddy and climb trees, while girls are told to stay
safe, to 'be careful'. If a boy falls over and skins his knee, he's
told to get on with it, while girls are more likely to be coddled.

We're praised for being 'good girls', but because 'boys will be boys', they're expected to be more unruly.

Being protected against failure like this, we don't learn to handle things in the way that's expected of boys. In numerous ways, we don't develop the confidence to cope with challenges because Mum and Dad are always there to scoop us up and keep us safe. Of course, this doesn't apply to every girl, but it could partially explain why the millennial generation of women struggles so much with a fear of failure and with low self-esteem.

Rejection may be a biggie for you – it is for lots of us. Rejection is the ultimate fear because we make it mean that we are not enough; we've done something wrong, displeased another person or not been good enough. We take rejection as a sign that we're unworthy or unlovable. And we are ultra-sensitive to it. Women's leadership coach Homaira Kabir told Forbes: '[Women's] fears are far more about rejection than they are about failure. Subtle shifts in mood, lack of adequate approval or an uninviting stance can make some women feel small or doubtful starting at a very young age, causing them to go to extreme lengths to avoid those feelings as often as possible without rational awareness of why they may be doing so.'[1] Who else feels as though they are highly attuned to the slightest facial expression that might suggest displeasure or irritation in another person? Having been raised to please others, it's especially painful when we feel we haven't.

Rejection reframes

Hands up who's ever experienced rejection? Oh, that's 100 per cent of us then!

Who's heard the following?

- 'I like you, I just don't want a relationship right now.'
- 'We went with another candidate for the job.'
- 'Things just got serious with Jen, so I can't see you again.'
- 'We're going to pass on your offer, I'm afraid.'

I have an impressive track record when it comes to being rejected by men. I was seventeen when the boy I *thought* was my forever-boyfriend (I mean, what did I know?) took me to the corner of the pub and solemnly told me, 'I like you, I just don't want a relationship.'

It stung like hell. His words ricocheted around my head and I walked around with a heavy, dull ache in my heart for months. As a highly insecure teenager, his words seemed to confirm what I'd always feared was true, that I was never going to be good enough. Not for him . . . and not for anyone else.

My brain searched for evidence from my past to support the belief of my unworthiness. I remembered feeling 'abandoned' by Dad when he worked away for weeks at a time. I recalled the look of disgust on a classmate's face, after I'd planted an unwelcome kiss on his cheek in Year 4. Oh, and there was the guy I liked in Year 7 who only had eyes for my best friend. This pattern continued into my late teens and early twenties.

Let's be honest – rejection sucks. If you've ever felt slapped in the face by it (and we all have) it won't be too much of a surprise when I tell you rejection activates the same areas of the brain as physical pain. It's no wonder we try and avoid it at all costs!

We try so many ways to contort and limit ourselves in the name of avoiding the agony of being rejected. Just some of them: people pleasing, saying yes to things we don't want, keeping quiet about how we actually feel and holding ourselves back.

But the truth is, rejection is not all that it seems. Rejection itself isn't so bad. It's the *meaning* we give to it that is.

Because when you're rejected, most of the time you won't actually have lost anything.

You didn't have the guy before, and you don't now.

You didn't have the job before and you still don't have it now.

You can't have something taken away from you that was never yours in the first place. The only thing you've lost is an idea, a story. Even if you thought you had a future with that person or career path, that's still just a story.

What's the 'meaning' that you're giving to the rejection?

Your Tinder date doesn't ask for a second date . . . so you tell yourself you'll be single forever (and that you're basically unlovable).

You view seven flats you found on SpareRoom.com and each one gets filled by someone else . . . so you tell yourself everyone must hate the sight of you.

You make twenty-two sales calls and don't manage to close any . . . so you tell yourself you're rubbish at your job and are bound to get fired.

The first part of each of these sentences may be fact, but it's the second part – the story you make up about the rejection – that hurts, and is usually pure fiction.

I'm not trying to make light of the real pain you might be experiencing if you've just lost your job or been left by your partner. But you can bet the story you tell yourself about what has happened has the power to make you feel much worse – or to empower you to make the best of a bad situation.

With that in mind, here are some simple ways to soothe the pain of rejection.

Tell yourself a new story

Success coach Jack Canfield has a saying: 'Some Will, Some Won't, So What? Someone's Waiting.' He calls it the 4 SW's. What he's saying is that some people are going to say yes, and some are going to say no. And so what! Out there somewhere, someone is waiting for you and your ideas. Every no gets you closer to a yes, it's just a matter of time. So ask yourself:

- How can I apply this to my situation?
- What other empowering stories could I tell myself about what happened?
- Am I making space for something even better?
- Am I clearing my calendar for new opportunities?
- Am I going to come out of this experience stronger and wiser?
- What would my best friend say about this? What would Beyoncé [or insert your female role model] do?

'No' will eventually lead you to a better place

In an episode of the Tim Ferriss podcast, Maria Sharapova, one of the world's highest paid female athletes, opens up about rejection. And guess what? She doesn't believe in it. Her father taught her that a 'no' opens you up to other opportunities. She advises that we 'turn a no into something that brings you to a better place'.

No may bring you one step closer to a yes, or it can help

you adjust your approach or change to a better direction. Either way, it's just a bump in the road, not a dead end.

Remember your tribe

We evolved to feel the pain of rejection for a reason. Remember I explained how, when we were cavewomen, being ostracized by the tribe was a life or death situation? We evolved to avoid rejection. That shit is hard-wired!

But now? It's an out-of-date, evolutionary leftover because even if you lose a friend through an argument or growing apart, it may be sad, but it's not a threat to your survival. And thankfully, most of us have our own tribe of friends and family who love and accept us no matter what.

So spend some time reminding yourself of how warm, lovable, frickin' hilarious and irreplaceably gorgeous your friends and family think you are, to soothe that out-of-date rejection fear. Spend time with people you love, reach out and ask for help, send out an SOS to your WhatsApp group of besties and remember that you are loved beyond belief. I'll talk more about connecting with your tribe in Chapter 38 'How to find your people'.

Everybody says no, sometimes

You say no to things all the time, I'll bet. You 'reject' things for a whole host of reasons, some rational, some totally random. If you've been rejected, often it's not personal, it doesn't mean you're bad, it's just down to the other person's preference. And that's A-OK.

I personally don't like certain varieties of things. I can't bear quinoa porridge (just no!), I can't wear nineties clothing (it never worked for me the first time around) and I don't find hairy chests attractive (luckily my current beau is as smooth as a dolphin). It's not to say these things aren't great for other people, they're just not my preference. My (not) boyfriend at seventeen showed he wasn't keen on the 'Chloe Brotheridge' variety of girlfriend. No problems there, really! It's just a preference. There are many, many would-be friends, lovers, clients and employers for whom you will be just their thing.

. . . .

Exercise: it's all just opinion

Tara Mohr, coach and author of *Playing Big*, offers a reframe to help us remember that everyone is disliked at some time or another. She suggests this:

Read the reviews of your favourite book on Amazon. Some will be rave reviews, others will be stinky ones or will seem mean, illogical or random.

Realize that even if an author is world class, there will always be people who 'reject' them and their work. Even though you love the book, others will hate it – and there could be a million reasons why. It doesn't make the book 'bad'; it's all just opinion. It's impossible to please everyone.

Now repeat: IT'S IMPOSSIBLE TO PLEASE EVERY-ONE.

. . . .

What would your BFF (or your mum) say?

How would they answer back to that rejection story you've been telling yourself?

If you find yourself, post-rejection, reeling into 'no-one-will-ever-love-me-I'm-terrible-at-my-job-and-will-die-alone-surrounded-by-cats' type thinking, consider what rational, loving and wise words a friend or family member would have to say about the situation.

Oh, and they're right!

You can't please everyone, all of the time

'I'd much rather be someone's shot of whiskey than everyone's cup of tea,' said Carrie Bradshaw in *Sex and the City*. Not everyone likes whiskey, but that's OK because for some people you are the absolute DREAM and they will savour you, cherish you, breathe you in and talk about you for many years to come.

Hold out to be someone's whiskey.

Summary

★ Because of how we're raised, women often fear failure more than men.

★ The story we tell ourselves about having been rejected is often the most painful part; but we can change the story.

★ It's impossible to please everyone, and we are all rejected at some point or another.

CHAPTER 17

How to embrace success

Our deepest fear is not that we are inadequate. Our
deepest fear is that we are powerful beyond measure.
It is our light, not our darkness that most frightens us.
We ask ourselves, 'Who am I to be brilliant, gorgeous,
talented, fabulous?' Actually, who are you not to be?
You are a child of God. Your playing small does not
serve the world. There is nothing enlightened about
shrinking so that other people won't feel insecure
around you. We are all meant to shine.

MARIANNE WILLIAMSON

When I'm talking about success, I'm not talking about reaching the top of the corporate ladder or winning *Britain's Got Talent*. Yes, success might mean those things, but it could also be the success of having a big group of friends or getting a pay rise at the shop you work in, or setting up your own small business.

What if the only thing scarier than failing is the possibility of seeing that you are pretty fucking amazing? Now, before you roll your eyes and brace yourself for a positivity pep talk that you'll likely reject out of hand, or before you get too much of an inflated ego, come closer and listen. What I mean is, everyone is special . . . and no one is special. You are exquisitely unique . . . and also just like everybody else. We are all, as human beings, amazing, miraculous and beautiful. The most complex and intelligent life in the known universe. The scary part is, if we knew how brilliant we were, we might actually have to go after the things we really want. The responsibility of being the one who can save and heal yourself (and the world) would feel too much. Or you might feel plain old unworthy of making your mark, finding it impossible to live up to your potential.

Last year, my career started to go really well. I was being given new opportunities, as more and more people wanted to know what I had to say. From the outside, I looked as if I was flying. But inside, I felt like slamming down on the brakes, crawling into a pillow fort with a tub of Ben & Jerry's and never coming out. I'd been comfortable doing what I knew before; and now it seemed I had to go outside my comfort zone every single day. Suddenly, speaking up, setting boundaries, saying no and 'being seen' became everyday occurrences.

The more exposure I was getting, the more I felt like hiding away. I found myself worrying, how can I keep this up? What if I end up getting overwhelmed and burning out? Will my friends think I'm getting 'too big for my boots'? I was concerned I couldn't sustain this extra level of pressure, that I'd end up falling from this greater height. I realized, being more 'visible' had left me more open to criticism, that people were more likely to offer up their unsolicited opinions or give me unwelcome feedback. It seemed much safer to stay within the confines of what I'd always done before. I realized that, like many women, I wasn't being held back by fear of failure but by my fear of success.

Success can be so scary

My friend Sophie wondered if workmates would still like her if she went after a promotion. My client Amber felt unworthy of sitting at the managers' table and feared 'being found out' as not good enough for her new, bigger role. With success comes heavier responsibility and higher pressure – and so, fears. These fears can be unconscious, can rear their heads to silently sabotage success just as we're starting to achieve some of the things we've wanted. Our unconscious fears can even trick us into thinking we don't really want success. They might make you purposefully act less confident than you feel, for fear of judgement, or make excuses for holding yourself back. They might tell you, you don't need to push through the discomfort and show up to that key event, it's fine to stay in and do your laundry!

Fear can even make you self-sabotage your success. Maybe you start a petty argument with your new partner after an amazing date because things were going a little too well and, underneath, it was making you uneasy. Or you find yourself getting too drunk at your birthday party because all the love and attention felt overwhelming, and you doubted whether you deserved it.

Success does look different for everyone but here are some examples that might reveal that you fear success:

- You don't prepare enough for your presentation because you're afraid if you smash it you'll be asked to present all the time.
- You continuously refresh your email and check your Facebook notifications when you should be working on your side hustle.
- You keep your achievements to yourself because you worry your friends will think you're 'boasting'.
- You don't ask for what you want at work or in a relationship, because you're scared about what will happen if you actually get it.

· ·

Exercise: **face your fears**

Write out each of your fears and their possible consequences by answering the following questions. Try to stay rational and be kind to yourself as you answer:

What is scary about being confident, assertive and successful?

What do I think the possible downsides of this success might be?

What are all the different, more positive and constructive ways I can handle this?

Consider these possible answers:

Friends thinking I'm getting over confident → They reject and abandon me → The likelihood is that they will be proud and happy for me and if they're not, do I really need them as friends?

Being asked to do more work → I end up burning out → I can stay aware of this and take action if and when it happens. I can take care of myself more. I can set firm boundaries, so I am not overworked.

Getting more praise → It makes me uncomfortable and embarrassed → I can work on accepting praise and compliments. If someone praises me, I deserve it! I can practise saying 'thank you' when someone pays me a compliment.

· ·

Summary

★ Our fear of success can sometimes be even bigger than our fear of failure.

★ Think about situations where you might be fearing success. Find a more proactive and rational way to look at each one.

CHAPTER 18

Find the courage to be imperfect

Success is not final, failure is not fatal: it is the
courage to continue that counts.
WINSTON CHURCHILL

Do you recognize yourself in any of these situations?

- You spend an hour rechecking an email that others might spend ten minutes on.
- You don't ask for help from friends or family because you feel you should have your shit together at all times.
- There's a dark cloud over your day because there's a tiny stain on your top.
- You fluffed a few words during a presentation, so you feel like a total loser.
- You fear you might have said 'the wrong thing' to a friend of a friend and now you can't stop beating yourself up.
- You can't delegate to other people because they 'just won't do it right'.

If you do, you might just be a perfectionist.

I've already described how perfectionism is an impossible goal, one that uses up valuable energy. Now I'd like to go further: I believe fear of failure (and of success) in women can be caught up with our need to be perfect. And becoming brave means needing to learn to have the courage to be imperfect.

As I mentioned in Chapter 10 'Shatter the illusion of perfectionism', many of us don't recognize ourselves as 'perfectionists' because we can see we're not totally perfect. But – and this is a big but – we do have perfectionist tendencies. This is something I see in clinic, time and again, the sense that failure, mistakes or weakness are unacceptable or a downright disaster.

Perfectionist tendencies keep us small. They stop us trying things unless we're 100 per cent sure we can succeed. And we don't ask for new opportunities because we don't feel 'ready'. Sure, there's nothing wrong with having high standards, but when they are so impossibly high that you never feel you're good enough to go after what you want, it's time for a perfectionism overhaul.

Let's start by looking at where your perfectionism may have come from. In school, achievement and high standards are rewarded. Being a perfectionist is often positively reinforced. Praise from parents can lead us to associate doing well with being loved. Maybe you were told what a 'good girl' you were, or parents and teachers said what a 'perfect' daughter or student you were. On the flipside, if you were pressured by critical parents when you were young, it might have caused you to grow up believing you're not good enough as you are and must always push to do better. And as society rewards physical attractiveness, looking impeccably well dressed or always having flawless nails and hair may have been reinforced for you too. In the present, perhaps a boss loves your extreme attention to detail and work ethic and now you feel pressured to keep it up.

When you're living in a place of not-enoughness, it doesn't matter what you achieve. Only when you are perfect will you feel ready to be your most confident self and do what you've dreamed of doing . . . but sadly you never feel perfect enough. Once you've achieved one goal, it won't be long before you're unhappy again, and start working towards the next goal. You see yourself and what you do in black and white, as either perfect or a failure. Relying on and attempting to control what other people think of you creates a lot of tension and means you can't relax and be yourself.

Lowering your standards

I had a client, Susannah, who was always striving for perfection in her work. But as soon as she'd attained a great result or reached a milestone, she set the bar higher. She was the youngest senior member of staff at her law firm, had bought a house way before most of her peers. She described herself as always giving 110 per cent, but never feeling worthy or good enough. She put huge amounts of pressure on herself to do and be more. She was the first person at her desk in the morning and the last person to leave.

Susannah was never going to reach a point where she could relax and enjoy even a tiny bit of her success. The idea of making a mistake or failing was so hideous to her, she had to keep every aspect of her job and public profile tightly under control. She used up massive amounts of energy trying to please her superiors and was terrified of saying the wrong thing. When something did go awry at work, she'd agonize about it for days and beat herself up.

When Susannah came to see me, she was suffering from panic attacks and regularly burst into tears in the toilets at work. She was convinced it was only her high standards that had kept her in the job for so long. I asked her, 'What are those high standards costing you?' She told me: sleepless nights, anxiety, and having no time to find a partner, among others. I suggested an experiment: for Susannah to lower her standards by just 10 per cent. This, she felt, was manageable and achievable.

She started to leave work earlier two nights a week, she began to delegate more, and she made a commitment to be kinder to herself about any perceived mistakes. It took courage for her to risk being imperfect, but as a result she felt calmer, happier and had more time to date and meet new people. To her surprise, she was still successful at work, and colleagues even commented that she seemed more relaxed and approachable.

The perfection myth

There are four lies that make up the perfection myth:

1. Perfection = happiness

'If I'm a perfect friend, then everyone will like me and I'll be happy.'

Everything we do as human beings is to try and increase our happiness. The only reason you want the perfect CV/partner/pair of jeans/yearly review is because you believe it will make you happy. It won't.

2. Perfection = readiness

'When I'm perfect at my role, then I'll be ready for a promotion.'

If you're waiting for perfect conditions or to be perfect at something, you'll never take the action that you want. Waiting to be perfect before you can accept yourself is deluded because it just isn't going to happen.

3. Perfection = confidence

'If I get top marks in my exams, then I'll be confident in a job interview.'

'When I'm a perfect mum, then people won't judge me.'

We believe we can't feel confident about our bodies unless they're perfect. Many of us are waiting for perfection before we accept and love ourselves or dare to go after the relationship, job or life that we want.

4. Perfection = achievable

'If my boss thinks I'm the perfect employee, then I'll finally be satisfied.'

I'd argue that perfection isn't achievable. Everyone has their own, different idea of what 'perfect' means. Being seen as perfect in the eyes of everyone is impossible.

The problem with the 'if-then' mindset is that trying to get to perfection puts a huge strain on you. Constantly being on edge, overworking, worrying and pressurizing yourself as you try to attain your goal is a sure-fire way to prevent yourself from feeling happy.

If you finally feel something might be perfect, your feelings of achievement are likely to be short-lived. That perfection won't last – it only takes some unexpected humidity to ruin a perfect hair day, or a delayed flight to spoil a perfect weekend away. Or else you immediately set your sights on the next goal. Just got a promotion? Start working towards the next one! Managed to squeeze into size eight jeans? Now you need to get down to a size six!

Think about this: what is perfection, anyway? In fact, it's

just someone's opinion! If it's your own, you'll know it changes depending on your mood and has probably changed over time too. If your version is about being perceived as perfect by another person, this fits firmly in the box marked 'things you can't control'. Hanging your happiness and confidence on your ability to control someone else's opinion is a recipe for misery. And if its pursuit makes you so anxious that you can't enjoy your life, what's the point?

Being human is messy. We are by our nature imperfect beings. Trying to be perfect actually goes against our nature! It's unnatural! What needs to come first is acceptance. Weirdly, that's when things start to feel perfect, when you accept that you, as you are, are pretty awesome. Accepting your imperfections doesn't mean stagnating. It's going to make your life so much richer to think of yourself as ever evolving, ever learning and growing, and always making progress, no matter what.

Embrace the mess

My client Anna told me about a summer trip to Amsterdam she'd organized for her mother and sister. She'd planned a stunning canal-side apartment, gallery visits and gorgeous places to eat and watch city life go by.

When they got to their Airbnb, Anna's mother pointed out the apartment was a bit smaller than expected and there weren't any tea bags. Being a perfectionist, Anna took this criticism to heart. It played on her mind, making her feel she'd failed. She continued to beat herself up all evening, so there was a tense atmosphere between the three of them.

Suddenly, just as they left the restaurant to walk back to the apartment, huge, heavy drops of summer rain began to fall. Since there were no taxis they had no choice but to make a run for it, getting soaked and arriving back tired but beaming with exhilaration. It was far from perfect, but they felt so present and alive. Afterwards, they all agreed that running home in the rain was the highlight of the trip!

Anna said, 'I realized it was only when I let go of perfect, just started to embrace the mess, that we ended up having the best time.'

If you can be brave enough to embrace life's imperfections and your own too, you open yourself up to enjoy things you didn't know you could.

The acceptance/perfection paradox

An interesting thing happens when you accept things as they are. Accepting just means being open to feeling that everything is OK, even if it doesn't go exactly to plan. And don't worry, this won't stop you doing your best or making progress. Accepting, rather than perfecting, is what leads to happiness and peace. Remind yourself of this: life feels perfect when you accept things as they are.

. . . .

Exercise: how to embrace flaws, mistakes and failures

Exercise 1: Find a way to reframe mistakes you may have made in the past by thinking about what you learned from them. How can you use what you learned to be better next time?

Exercise 2: List the ways or situations in which you are a perfectionist. Are you thinking in black and white or catastrophizing? How could you see things differently?

Find the courage to be imperfect

What would a good friend advise you to do? Are there ways to lower your standards to 'good enough' and to accept enough being enough, so you can move forward?

Exercise 3: List all of the benefits you'll get from being less of a perfectionist. They might be things such as, 'I'll be kinder to myself', 'I'll get more done', 'I'll be able to move forward and take action', 'I'll feel more confident', 'I'll embrace myself as I am' or 'I'll feel less anxious and stressed'.

. . . .

Exercise: **failing on purpose**

Sometimes we fear failure because we've never had a chance to fail and learn that it's OK. I'm going to suggest you make small mistakes on purpose. While this might seem excruciating at first, it really is the best way to learn that mistakes are, in fact, no big deal. I'm not suggesting you fail massively by sabotaging an important pitch at work. What we're looking for is a small, token failure. Try one of these or make up your own:

Leave a long silence during a presentation.

Purposely turn up late to a meeting.

Bake a wonky cake for a friend.

Wear something mismatched to the office.

You'll discover that not only will you survive, but no one will care much and you'll be less worried about failing in the future.

. . . .

Summary

★ Many people have perfectionist tendencies. Even if you have a messy desk, you can still be a perfectionist in other areas.

★ Perfection is a myth; it doesn't exist, it doesn't lead to happiness, and 'being perfect' won't lead to you feeling more confident.

★ Things feel perfect when we embrace the messiness of life (and ourselves!) as it is.

CHAPTER 19

Why failure is an option

> Sometimes courage looks a lot like failure.
> **JESSICA LAHEY, *THE GIFT OF FAILURE***

Here are some of the world's most famous 'failures', those who tried and tried again until they hit the big time or created something that changed the world.

- Beyoncé's first singing group, Girls Tyme, lost the US TV talent competition *Star Search*.
- Katy Perry had two failed record deals before her third deal with Columbia led to success with 'I Kissed A Girl'.
- J. K. Rowling's *Harry Potter and the Philosopher's Stone* was rejected by twelve publishers before being accepted.
- One year into her contract, Marilyn Monroe was dropped by 20th Century Fox for being 'unattractive'.
- Oprah was fired from her first job co-anchoring the news.
- Lady Gaga was dropped by Def Jam records after only three months.

OK, you get the picture. Failure happens to everyone. Failing is an inevitable by-product of doing. Perhaps what's holding you back from being all you can be, is your worry about making mistakes.

When I started out as a therapist eight years ago, I knew I wanted to run group workshops, but kept putting it off. Finally, I decided I had to do it. I put in weeks of promotion, posting up my home-made flyers in every cafe in Hackney, doing a Facebook advert and sending emails to past clients to drum up business.

On the day, a grand total of one paying person showed up, the numbers made up by friends and my sister. I was pretty embarrassed, in fact devastated. That evening, as I tidied away the yoga mats and gathered pens and paper, I nearly cried. I thought people's lack of interest was evidence I was useless as a therapist, nobody liked me, and I should give up on workshops as they were never going to work.

After dwelling in self-loathing and misery for an hour or so, I decided to do some journaling. As I started to write down my thoughts, I realized I'd been lost in catastrophic black and white thinking. I had believed that if the workshop wasn't a triumph, it was an utter disaster.

I made a list of all of the ideas I could think of to make it more successful next time. I decided to reframe the whole experience as a source of valuable feedback; a great starting point from which I could improve.

Planning the next workshop, I made sure I used that list. I invited people in person. I was more confident in the emails I sent out and in talking about the benefits of coming. I reached out to my network for help. And guess what? I got a very respectable ten people to attend. As life coach and business strategist Tony Robbins says, 'There's no such thing as failure, only results.' Whatever happens, it's useful information.

What meaning do you give to your 'failures'? Do you take them personally, believing failing means there's something wrong with you, that you are uniquely flawed and destined for a life of disappointment? If so, you need to challenge that belief. Because it is impossible for a person to be a failure. There are so many factors that make up the complete you, a human being. Failures in no way define you.

Our minds love to make things binary: sink or swim, win or lose, feeling like you can take on the world or the world is against you. It can seem as though there is no in between; and obviously this is irrational. Life is constantly moving, changing and growing, in flux. To think that we'll one day arrive at a state of failure (or even success!) can't be true. What you might see as failure is just a pause on the twisting, turning path of life, a pivot on the way to the next thing. You can transform the meaning you give to failure from 'I'm not good enough' all the way to 'an important stepping stone on the path to my success'.

Even companies that seem unstoppable now, like Apple and Instagram, will one day 'fail'. We talk about a relationship 'failing' but is that really true because it ended? Maybe it was good for a time, perhaps you learned a lot or it paved the way for your next relationship?

The truth is, failure is an essential part of growing and learning. You were born with an inbuilt ability to try things, fail and try again. It's human nature. Think about when you were really little, learning to walk. One day you pulled yourself up, took a tiny step . . . then tumbled over. Day after day, you stood up, tried to walk and fell over. Each time you became a little stronger, wiser and more coordinated. You didn't allow the falls to hold you back, because instinctively you knew they were all part of the process. Learning to walk without falling over is impossible. Failure is inevitable. But know this; as you fail, you get better and better.

As an adult, you may have forgotten that it's OK to fail, but you can re-learn how. If you don't even try, you fail by default. Anxiety, about perfection and making mistakes, leading to procrastination and not taking chances, can hold you back from success. If that's true for you, the answer is to take a tiny step in the right direction. Make a start (the most important bit!) and the momentum will grow along with your confidence.

· ·

Exercise: take a micro-bravery step

Make a list of the things you're afraid to do because of perfectionism or fear of failure. What is one small, teeny, tiny step you could take towards the thing you're afraid to do? It could be:

Spending thirty minutes researching a new project.

Deciding what you're going to say in a tricky conversation.

Sending an email to set up a meeting.

By taking one, small, brave step forwards, you'll build your courage to take bigger steps and grow your momentum to move forward.

· ·

Being vulnerable is beautiful

Did you know your imperfections could make you more attractive, not less? A psychological phenomenon – brilliantly named the Pratfall Effect – says if you are seen as competent and yet you make a small mistake, such as fluffing a few words in a presentation or dropping a drink, it can make others perceive you as more likeable.

The same holds true when you admit to a weakness or your imperfections, and so reveal your authentic self. People are more likely to warm to you; we prefer fallible over too-perfect-to-be-real. I'm sure you can think of people you know whose faults and vulnerabilities make you love them all the more. In the celebrity world, the people we fall in love with are often the ones just being themselves, imperfections and all: Jennifer Lawrence for her goofyness in interviews; Chrissy Teigen for tweeting pictures of her cellulite and stretch marks; and Lena Dunham for her vulnerable shares about mental health.

All those things you pressurize yourself about? The people who really matter don't give a damn about them. When I think of my beloved friends and family, I know their material success, career progression or even their ability (or inability) to apply perfect eyeliner don't affect how much I love them one bit. You are loved for who you are, as you are.

From perfection to progress

Choose curiosity over fear.

LIZ GILBERT

Because reaching perfection is at best a strain and at worst impossible, focus instead on progress. See yourself as ever-evolving and changing. And remember your worth does not depend on how well you do. Be gentle with yourself and know that you are here to learn and grow, not to be perfect. When you do your best and learn from your mistakes, it is always good enough.

Some people believe that the opposite of fear is not courage or relaxation, but curiosity. Fear makes us feel like running away, while curiosity makes us move towards. Fear keeps us stuck, while curiosity wants us to explore.

The language you use is important here. In recent years, when I've felt myself falling into fear, I've shifted my perspective on the situation with language. Instead of the adrenaline-drenched 'what if . . . ?' I've started to use a light and breezy 'I wonder what . . . ?'.

This simple reframe allows you to approach things with interest rather than trepidation, with openness rather than catastrophization, and with excitement rather than dread. Can you ask, 'I wonder what . . . ?' and get curious about that tough conversation, how your new relationship will unfold or how much money your side-business will make this year?

What could go right?

Have you noticed how things tend to turn out OK, most of the time? Many of us focus too much on what could go wrong, not enough on what could go right. When you enter a situation with openness and an expectation that all will be well, your mind is in the best state for that to be so. When you're fearful, blood flow gets directed away from the frontal cortex, the rational part of your brain, towards the amygdala and other parts of the body, to prepare you to run away or fight. So being scared and doubtful means you're less rational and clear thinking . . . therefore less equipped to handle whatever happens. When you're thinking positively, you're also more likely to feel confident.

. . . .

Exercise: rehearse for success

Think of an upcoming tricky conversation, one where you might fail. Perhaps you need to set a boundary with someone, want to ace a project at work, or ask for what you want in a relationship. Mentally rehearse it going exactly as you want. Use all your senses to imagine it going well; your confident posture, your clear and calm speaking voice, you being 100 per cent present, feeling assertive and self-assured. Do this repeatedly and you'll create positive expectation and, eventually, a new self-image that will take you into the situation with new confidence.

. . . .

Exercise: **facing fear of failure**

If you imagine the worst happening, you can also imagine how you would deal with it. That will set up your inner confidence that you can cope, no matter what happens. Answer these questions:

What failure am I afraid of, right now?

What could happen if I did fail?

How exactly would I handle this?

Summary

★ Turn your failures into useful information to help you improve.

★ Taking small, micro-brave steps helps to build your confidence.

★ Choosing curiosity over fear helps you to move towards things rather than running away.

PART FIVE

How to heal shame and self-doubt

CHAPTER 20

Bringing shame into the light

The greatest act of courage is to be and to own all of
who you are—without apology, without excuses,
without masks to cover the truth of who you are.

DEBBIE FORD, *COURAGE*

'Do you believe all human beings are generally valuable and worthwhile?' my therapist asked me.

'Yes, of course,' I answered.

'So what's so special about you?' she said, raising an eyebrow.

'Huh,' I said, as the penny dropped.

Like most of us, I believe all human beings are valuable and worthwhile. I am a human being. Therefore, I should believe I am valuable too. I felt a crack appear in my hardened emotional shell and a shard of light rushed in. And that light began to dissolve my shame.

I mulled over this for days. Was I 'so special' that I alone was truly a bad and worthless human being? Or was I just as good and valuable as any other human being?

We've all been in situations which could lead us to feel ashamed, whether you recognize it or not. We've all been ignored, rejected or told off. Some of us have even been abused. Whether we develop shame or not as a result depends on the meaning we gave these experiences. We experience shame when we believe, not that we did something wrong, but that we are bad and wrong.

Shame is a deep-rooted cause of a lot of our suffering.

Shame suffocates self-esteem and, along with it, confidence. Shame tells you, 'There is something wrong with you, you're not good enough, you're worthless.' Shame tells you, you are uniquely flawed, broken and unfixable. But I promise you, this is not true. And I also promise you, you can heal shame.

Shame often has its roots in childhood. Our developing brains can't comprehend the context, the bigger picture or the true meaning of what happened. As children we take things personally – we believe that things that happen are our fault, without understanding the bigger picture.

I uncovered how shame had taken root in me, during therapy in my early twenties. At one point during my very first session, I looked down and saw I was clawing at my jean-clad legs. I would have done anything to distract myself from the butt-clenching discomfort and awkwardness of having to do what felt almost impossible: talk about my feelings. Each time the therapist asked me a question, I'd feel a grey mist of confusion descend over me, so I couldn't even access my own thoughts or emotions.

Now, I realize this was my protection mechanism, the shell I'd grown to prevent my personal sense of shame being exposed. Shame loves a secret. It causes us to keep things inside so that you don't have to feel vulnerable. In a world where projecting a perfect image is the norm, being seen for all that you are is scary as hell.

Since my teenage years, I'd noticed this underlying sense I wasn't good enough. It felt as if I'd been wired up wrongly. I had a deep sense of awkwardness, that I never quite fitted in. I'd get easily embarrassed. I wasn't at home in myself. I later discovered all these feelings have one name: shame. Looking back, I now realize that this was partly due to the fact that, as a sensitive child, I'd internalized getting told off by my parents and misinterpreted it as 'I am bad'.

Apparently, shame had an evolutionary purpose; again it was about helping us to fit into the tribe by following the rules. Daniel Sznycer, psychologist and lead author of a 2016 study into the evolutionary basis for shame says, 'The function of pain is to prevent us from damaging our own tissue. The function of shame is to prevent us from damaging our social relationships, or to motivate us to repair them.'[1]

However, most of the shame we experience now is toxic. This evolutionary survival mechanism no longer serves us. Many people didn't grow up in families that encouraged talking about feelings, or in a society that teaches self-love and acceptance. So our shame is left to fester.

Is it shame or guilt?

Shame and guilt are both hard emotions to take. The words are often used together but, in fact, they have very different meanings. And very different effects, too.

Guilt is when you feel bad about having done something you think was wrong. It can be a helpful emotion since it encourages us to change our behaviour or make amends.

Shame is the feeling that you, as a person, are bad, wrong, broken or irredeemable. Rotten. A disgrace! It's the epitome of not-enoughness that is the root of much of our anxiety, depression and lack of confidence. It's linked to low self-esteem, addiction and even aggression. It is much less useful than guilt. In fact, I'd go so far as to say, it's one of the most destructive human emotions, the one that holds us back the most.

Shame stings. It feels like a dark, heavy weight. And so many of us lug it around with us. When you carry this heavy burden, your powers are dampened down. You don't realize how good you are, and so you don't even try. You're scared to ask because you don't believe you deserve a 'yes', and you can't handle a 'no'. You don't believe you're worthy of the things you want. You don't feel good enough to go for your dreams. Playing the shame story on a loop makes you less resilient, less capable and less 'you'. It's hard to be authentically yourself when you think that the real you is broken and unacceptable.

Where shame comes from

Shame arises when something you've done – or something you are – is judged to be 'bad', so you blame yourself (or are blamed), and then you internalize that judgement. It's a chain:

Event → You get judged or blame yourself
→ You internalize 'I am bad' → Shame

I'll give you an example from my own life. When I was ten years old I was a bridesmaid at the beautiful garden wedding of my aunt. At one point, my grandma and another male guest seemed to beckon me over. I ran over to them, and the man said, 'Oh, sorry, we were actually calling the cat over.' I was MORTIFIED. How could I have thought they wanted to speak to me? What's wrong with me? I'm so stupid, I berated myself. Instead of dismissing this as a simple mistake, I felt I'd not only made the mistake of running over, but also been rejected. The result? I experienced shame. What appears so insignificant now has stayed with me because of the meaning I gave it.

Shame also arises as an adult, but it's often the early experiences that stick with us the longest. Experiences that result in shame can be big and traumatic, such as abuse or abandonment: shame happens when the person takes on board the belief that it is somehow their fault. Or it can come from experiences that seem small, like me at the wedding, or from being shouted at by your (still very loving) parents. You can feel shame even when the situation is entirely not your fault or an unintentional mistake, for example if you peed your pants aged five and it was met with an eye roll and a 'not again!'. While abuse can have the biggest impact, don't let the seeming insignificance of your experience shame you into feeling shame about feeling shame – you feel how you feel, and it's important not to compare your experience to someone else's.

While some people will recognize a shame-creating moment, because it will have stuck in their mind, vividly, for others it might still be unconscious. You might find that when you think about it, the moment will still feel charged with emotion. You may find it painful – as I did – to even go there. Whenever an experience is of high emotional intensity, it forms a strong memory and any associated beliefs may take root in our unconscious mind. It will take courage to look at these experiences, but it's necessary if we want to heal and transform.

If you've been the victim of abuse, be it sexual, physical, mental or emotional, I strongly encourage you to seek professional help. You don't have to deal with this alone – treatment is often successful at helping people process and move past what they have experienced.

This is a memory of feeling shamed that has stuck with me: I was aged ten when my teacher devised a game based around the times tables. The class would start off sitting in our chairs, and we'd each be asked a times table question – say, six times seven. If we got the answer right, we could go up a level, first by standing up, then standing on our chair, then up on the desk. If we got it wrong, we had to go down, sitting on the floor, then lying on it. Despite a fair amount of very frustrating practice, I was never very good at times tables, so each time I'd end up lying on the dirty floor, amongst the dust and pencil sharpenings, feeling humiliated. With all the other children, literally, looking down on me.

The message I was receiving was, 'You're stupid and not good enough, so you should lie in dirt.' I'm sure this wasn't the teacher's intention, but the young mind takes things personally. My shame told me: you are not smart enough. And during my early adulthood I'd constantly doubt my intelligence, despite getting great marks at school and university.

There is an endless list of potential situations that can lead to shame, but here are some examples:

Abandonment – you were looked after by different family members a lot because your mum wasn't able to for much of the time due to mental illness; you felt it was your fault she was ill.

Abuse – your dad would threaten to kill himself and he would blame you for burdening his life.

Neglect – your parents were often so busy with work there was little time for you.

Having a parent hit you or shout at you in public.

Being bullied at school.

Growing up in poverty while many of your school friends were well-off.

Showing your family a dance that you just learned and someone snapped, 'Don't be such a show-off!'

Being told you're stupid, arrogant or a know-it-all by the teacher, in front of the whole class.

Being ignored by a family member as you try to show them your latest finger painting.

Your dad never hugging you or telling you that he loved you.

Walking along the high street with your family and someone shouting racist abuse at you.

Turn the light on

If we can share our story with someone who responds with empathy and understanding, shame can't survive.

BRENÉ BROWN, *DARING GREATLY*

If all of this sounds pretty dark, don't worry, because shame can be healed. Babies aren't born with shame. They seem instinctively to know they are lovable. Their smiles are designed to melt any heart. They're not shy about asking for what they need, loudly expressing themselves and demanding all the attention is on them, as any sleep-deprived new parent will know. Shame is something we learn – and the good news is, we can unlearn it.

Starting to work through your shame can feel a little like being scared of a monster in the dark; you don't know what's there but you're too scared to switch on the light for fear of what you might see. But when you do switch on the light and look, you realize there was nothing there anyway. Nothing to see here! Just a human being, doing their best.

I'm going to teach you how to turn on that light and shine it into every corner, so that you can see that the shame monster isn't so scary, in fact it's made up.

I'll never forget my first experiences of the power of being seen, heard and accepted as I shared my shame. Sitting in a circle with other women, we'd each share our experiences of anxiety. All of us had gone to dark places in our minds. The feelings of worthlessness and isolation; believing that we were the only ones to feel that way, while everyone else was 'sorted'. Women who hated their appearance so much that it had stopped them from socializing. Those who felt lonely and disconnected even when in a crowded room. As I and others talked, I noticed the nods of recognition that silently said 'me too'. I saw the relief on people's faces as they realized they weren't alone, the surprise that everyone in the room had felt the same 'not good enoughness'. I felt the comfort of knowing I wasn't as uniquely messed up as I'd once thought.

Shame can't survive in the light of someone else's acceptance. This is another reason why therapy, talking to a friend and sharing in a circle are so powerful when it comes to healing the parts of us that hold us back.

. . . .

Exercise: list your shame triggers

Shame from the past often reaches out and latches on to the present. What you feel shame for now will often link back to your earlier life. Make a list of all the things you feel shame about. Writing them down and seeing them in black and white can help you to see them in perspective; they might even seem quite ridiculous, such as some of my examples below. For each one you write, imagine it's a friend telling you it as if they were experiencing it, and what you'd say to her or him. This will help you start to view yourself with kindness and compassion.

Bringing shame into the light

Ridiculous things I have felt shame about (to name but a few):

Pooing at festivals.

Pooing in general.

Being seen with no make-up.

Being seen naked by my boyfriend.

Running for the train at Manchester Piccadilly, missing it, then being seen to be disappointed (must be cool . . . must be cool!).

Being seen to be bothered about getting dumped (I was bothered).

Really trying to nail the moves at a dance class . . . and failing.

Smiling back at a good-looking guy who was smiling at someone else, not me.

Going in for a hug when my friend's friend was expecting a handshake.

Being myself.

Not being able to escape from my own wet-haired reflection while at the hairdresser.

Experiencing social anxiety.

Embarrassing things I did while drunk that I refused to hear about but included kissing inappropriate people or having drunken arguments (fingers in ears *la la la la la*).

. . . .

Summary

★ Shame is feeling 'I am bad' or 'I'm not good enough' and it often has its roots in childhood.

★ Shame can't survive being spoken. When we share our shame stories and bring them into the light, the shame starts to dissolve.

CHAPTER 21

How to heal shame and trauma

In Chapter 1 'Why I wrote this book for women', I mentioned trauma and how all of us will experience big 'T' or little 't' traumas in our lives. Trauma in childhood often leads to shame because undeveloped minds can't understand the full context, so conclude we are to blame. A distressing experience we haven't been able to fully process or overcome can be a trauma that leads to shame.

. . . .

Exercise: identify your shame stories

Which experiences in your life resulted in you blaming your-self and feeling not good enough or unworthy? In a notebook, write down these shame stories. If it feels too uncomfortable to write them on paper – and it can – you can type them into a computer, and either password protect the content or delete it afterwards.

. . . .

Exercise: give love and compassion to the ashamed part of yourself

This can be very healing. Imagine you are speaking to the younger you, at the time you experienced a particular shame event. Or you can write a letter to her. Let her know it's not her fault. What can you explain to her that she doesn't understand or is misinterpreting? What kind words can you say to her? What does she need to know? What advice do you have for her? Send her forgiveness, acceptance and love.

Here is what I wrote to my five-year-old self, who felt getting told off by her parents meant she was bad.

Dear five-year-old Chloe

Your parents love you so much. They get stressed and angry for their own reasons and it isn't really your fault. Everyone gets told off at times, and it doesn't mean you are bad. You don't need to be perfect, you're actually pretty great just as you are.

Mum and Dad sometimes get sad or angry but it always passes and soon, they'll be happy again. You are a good girl. Everything is going to be OK.

. . . .

The healing power of self-compassion

Self-compassion is simply being kind to yourself, as you would be to a good friend. It's so simple and yet it's hard to do. But it gets more natural and automatic with practice.

If you're experiencing shame or feelings of unworthiness right now, you'll probably need to remind yourself to do it repeatedly, at first. Download the self-compassion meditation in the bonuses at www.calmer-you.com/brave-bonus.

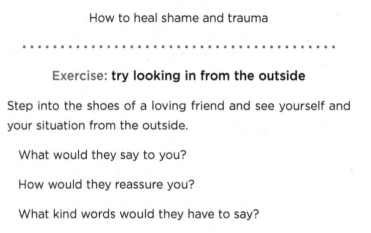

Exercise: try looking in from the outside

Step into the shoes of a loving friend and see yourself and your situation from the outside.

What would they say to you?

How would they reassure you?

What kind words would they have to say?

Prove the shameful belief wrong

Find evidence to the contrary of the shameful belief. So, I believed for a long time I wasn't clever enough, due in part to that times table 'game' above, and also from teachers believing I was dyslexic because my spelling was so poor (I wasn't). To start to change this belief, I've gathered evidence that this is not, in fact, true.

My evidence list goes like this:

- I've set up a successful business.
- I've helped hundreds of clients.
- I've written a bestselling book.

I can find plenty of other things to suggest the 'I am not smart enough' belief isn't true.

These days I tell myself the opposite: 'I am smart enough.' And I remember all the reasons that *this* is true.

What new, empowering belief can you create and what evidence can you list that this is true?

Feel it to heal it

*Unexpressed emotions will never die. They are buried
alive and will come forth later in uglier ways.*

SIGMUND FREUD

In her book *It's Not Always Depression*, therapist Hilary Jacobs
Hendel shares that shame is a 'defence emotion' that we use
when we don't want to feel other core emotions such as anger
and sadness. It protects us against having to feel those deeper
feelings, stops us having to process them and stops us being
vulnerable. Shame works because it allows us to avoid, change
the subject, keep quiet, ignore or look the other way.

In a world where 'good vibes only' is our motto and 'positive thinking' is prescribed as the cure-all for our emotions,
negative feelings get a bad rap. But stuffing down, numbing
and trying to ignore or mask our uncomfortable emotions
never works. Think of your feelings as having energy; if you
keep them inside, they stay stuck and will eventually come out
in ways that you don't want.

What happens when we don't feel our painful or uncomfortable feelings? Hilary Jacobs Hendel suggests when
emotions don't get processed, they stay stuck in our bodies
and lead to feelings that don't shift, such as depression and
anxiety. We've all done this kind of avoidance; we drown our
emotions by quaffing large glasses of white wine, inhaling
Domino's or rinsing our credit cards on Asos (I know it's not
just me). Even overthinking is a way of numbing ourselves
against having to feel.

But if we anaesthetize ourselves from our emotions, we can
never truly heal.

That energy needs to move through the body. Hilary
describes how to do this, by focusing on the emotions as they

come up. When you put your attention on the feeling, whether it's shame, fear, anxiety, anger, sadness, you stimulate the nerves that hold the feeling to move the emotions.

Next time you feel a negative emotion, before you reach for the Oreos, put all of your attention on to it. Allow yourself to dive into the emotion as you breathe deeply. If it's anger, pound on the sofa, stamp your feet and pound your fists in the air, or scream into a pillow (don't knock it until you've tried it). Feel the sadness fully, let the tears flow. Absorb yourself in the feeling of fear. You may be astounded to notice that when you permit yourself to feel fully, the emotions seem to pass through. If you can be brave enough to handle the feelings intensely for a few moments, you'll likely find some relief. Remind yourself that whatever you're feeling is OK and breathe through the intensity.

A client, Rebecca, told me recently, 'I got into an argument with my best friend about her not being able to make it to my birthday celebrations. I felt myself starting to spiral into shame, that I wasn't lovable or acceptable. It felt very similar to a feeling I'd had at school, aged thirteen, when my group of friends stonewalled me for a week for seemingly no reason.

At the time, it felt like the world was ending. We made friends again, but the fear that I was a bad friend stayed with me. I decided to try your technique of focusing on the feelings of shame and of not being loved. I felt myself well up, and I let out a few cries, but then I felt OK. It was like a wave rising up, crashing over me, and then the sea returning to calm again.'

The connection cure

In his book *Lost Connections*, Johann Hari has written about the roots of depression and his belief that connection is a cure for shame. Telling someone else what it is you're ashamed about – sharing your story, shining a light on it – and being accepted anyway is how you overcome shame. As Brené Brown so famously said, 'Shame can't survive being spoken.'

Having therapy took away a lot of my shame. The things that felt so painful and hideous to me, once said out loud and met with acceptance, lost their sting. Opening up to my boyfriend, Aidan, and being loved despite all the things I'd felt were so bad about me, took that shame away too. Sharing in a circle with others and learning that we all, deep down, struggle, was comforting and reassuring. I'll talk more about connection in Chapter 35 'How to grow your social confidence', and discuss how to cultivate the sense of community, openness and sharing that's so crucial for our self-esteem.

. . . .

Exercise: share your shame stories

Find a compassionate and loving person – a friend, partner, family member, therapist or support group – who you can share your shame stories with. Remember that shame can't survive being spoken.

. . . .

Finding your authenticity

All of the exercises in this chapter will help you to be more you. There is something incredibly liberating about accepting yourself for the beautiful mess that you are. Authenticity is about saying yes to all of who you are, to all parts of you: the imperfect parts, the broken parts and the rejected parts. When you can love the unlovable parts of yourself, that's freedom.

Self-acceptance is a superpower, it amplifies all of your abilities, makes you brave so nothing can hold you back.

Being authentic isn't something that you become, learn or cultivate. It's who you are, it's already there. Your job is simply to peel back the layers that have kept the real you hidden. You don't learn authenticity, you unlearn all the stuff that's held you back from it.

Summary

★ Give love and compassion to the ashamed part of yourself.

★ Always question your negative beliefs; they're never true.

★ When we feel our feelings fully, we allow ourselves to heal.

CHAPTER 22

Owning your shit

It wasn't me.

SHAGGY

To take your confidence to the next level, you'll need to come over to the dark side . . . your dark side, that is (don't worry, we all have one).

Knowing yourself in all your awfulness and all of your amazingness and knowing that it's all OK leads to a self-assurance that those who only focus on the good stuff, or feel ashamed of the bad stuff, cannot have. When we accept all of ourselves, the sparkly, shiny parts and the crappy ones, we're closer to finally feeling at home in ourselves.

While 'owning your shit' isn't technically a psychological term (although I think it should be), it is an important step when it comes to self-acceptance. Repressing and disowning our negative traits is one of the biggest things getting in the way of us loving and accepting ourselves. When we deny our dark side, we deny our very humanness. Psychiatrist Carl Jung called this part 'the shadow'. It's the bit we don't like to admit to, the bit we don't accept. But unless we embrace our darkness, we can't fully see our goodness. As Jung wrote, 'To confront a person with his shadow is to show him his own light.'

In a world where we're encouraged to strive for perfection, where 'positive thinking' is all the rage, and we're asked to spread good vibes at every opportunity, it can be hard to acknowledge our weaknesses, let alone accept them. But remember, it's normal to be imperfect, and only by accepting and, in fact, loving our imperfections, can we love our whole selves.

What is the dark side?

Often, it comes into being when we are shamed about a part of ourselves. And so we suppress that part and deny its existence, but it never goes away. A clue to your dark side is, it's what you want to hide, or deny, the parts that come with a fear of being found out.

I remember, in my first job after university, I was always finding excuses as to why there was a mistake in my work. I couldn't just own my mistake, apologize and get on with fixing it. I had to find an excuse for every mistake, why it wasn't my fault or why there was an excellent reason for it.

At home, I'd blame my boyfriend for the broken mug, conveniently forgetting it was me who put it into the dishwasher, or the scratch on the lino that could well have been my fault. I couldn't bear even to have made this kind of everyday mistake. I later realized the blame was me defending myself against the shame of 'being wrong'. At the time, accepting I could be wrong felt too painful.

This pattern kept me stuck. I couldn't get to know myself and accept all parts of myself while I was denying my imperfect, mistake-making part. I couldn't work on getting better because I wasn't able to recognize what the problem really was.

These days, I recognize my old pattern of avoiding being wrong by blaming other people, before it spirals. I've learned to acknowledge and take ownership of my mistakes. And it feels a lot more free and authentic.

There's another upside to loving all of you: having nothing to hide and knowing yourself, imperfections and all, makes what others think matter less. I don't have to be so afraid of people seeing 'the real me' because I'm accepting of all of the parts of myself.

Want to know an excellent way to find out what your shadow side is? Look at what annoys or upsets you about other people. Jung said we will often project our shadow on to someone else. When we notice something negative about another person, it's because we have that same quality. 'If you hate a person, you hate something in him that is part of yourself. What isn't part of ourselves doesn't disturb us,' writes Hermann Hesse.

In *Radical Forgiveness* Colin Tipping, founder of the Institute for Radical Forgiveness Therapy, puts it brilliantly: 'If you spot it, you've got it.' So if you find yourself spotting the arrogance, loudness or bossiness in another person, look for where that same quality hides in you, that you haven't accepted.

So, when another person causes you to eye-roll in their general direction, it's likely because they are reflecting back to you something you need to accept and love about yourself. If you're annoyed about the selfishness of another person, it could be because there's a selfish part within you that you're not acknowledging or accepting. It explains why I used to label outwardly confident women as 'show-offs'; I'd been shamed into suppressing the part of me that wanted to be the centre of attention, on a stage, inspiring other people or making them laugh (it's true).

Triggered by the colleague who's always dressed up for work like she's going to a wedding? Maybe it's because you don't feel worthy of 'standing out'.

Irked by the intern who's flirting with the guys in the office? Maybe it's because you desire attention too.

Pissed off at your friend who's always letting people walk all over her? In what ways do you allow yourself to get walked over?

. . . .

Exercise: your dark side list

Think about what triggers and annoys you about others, then use this to work out the qualities of your shadow side. Add to this the stuff you don't like to admit to, are ashamed of, that society doesn't deem 'acceptable' (hello, eating a sandwich over a waste-paper bin because you don't want to get crumbs everywhere).

Now ask yourself these questions:

How can I start to love and accept these parts, knowing they're part of what makes me human – and that they're the parts that need love the most?

How is the dark side of me trying to help me? Notice what good intentions your shadow parts have. They're there for a reason.

You don't need to justify the bad parts, just to bring acceptance to them so you can accept yourself. Carl Jung also said that 'what you resist, persists' and taught that when we can allow and accept something, it's easier for it to dissolve or transform. The energy of resistance keeps you stuck. It sounds counter-intuitive, but when you accept your faults, you'll find it makes them easier to change.

. . . .

Exercise: **identify the positive intentions**

With that list of your dark parts, write down what the positive intention behind each one is. For example:

I blame others because I can't stand to be 'wrong' →
This part of me is trying to protect me against feeling I'm 'bad'. It came from the shame I felt in the past when I'd get told off.

I'm controlling → Being in control feels safer. In the past, I've felt out of control and unsafe.

I'm selfish → If I'm not selfish, I'm scared my needs won't get met.

I'm rude → I have been taken advantage of in the past and I don't want it happening again.

I'm angry → My anger is to make right a perceived injustice.

I'm judgemental and I make assumptions → I believe that by putting others down I can make myself feel better and raise my own self-esteem.

I'm antisocial → It's conserving my energy and protecting me against the possibility of rejection.

. . . .

Knowing the positive intention of the shadow part allows us to decide whether it's serving us. If not, we can choose to change it or find another way to meet that need. For example, instead of being selfish as a means of trying to make sure your needs get met, can you instead try asking for what you want?

Instead of being judgemental about others, can you recognize your own need for validation and reassurance?

When we shine a light on the 'bad' parts of ourselves and recognize how they're trying to help us, we can start to accept them, integrate them and get to know ourselves on a deeper level. If we suppress or deny them, the shadow side only gets stronger. By bringing awareness to them, we have more control over them.

Owning your imperfections, accepting your whole self, all your mistakes, the gross bits and the messiness, will help you fully embrace yourself, be yourself and enjoy being you to the max. It's not easy to face your shadow, it takes courage for sure, but authentic, lasting confidence comes from knowing and accepting every part of ourselves. When we know ourselves, what others think starts to matter less. And we free ourselves to be the best we can be.

Summary

★ Getting to know and accept your dark side is the path to true self-acceptance.

★ There is often a positive intention behind the dark side; what is a healthier way to fulfil the positive intention?

★ If you spot it, you've got it. The parts of other people you find annoying are often those you have repressed and denied in yourself.

CHAPTER 23

Owning your body

In a society that profits from your self-doubt, liking
yourself is a rebellious act.
CAROLINE CALDWELL

We grew up in diet culture. Perhaps you watched your mother
going in and out of stints at WeightWatchers, obsessing over
points. Maybe she counted Slimming World Syns (eating is not
a sin, people!). Or weighed out precise portions of cardboard-
dry breakfast cereal like it was the most normal thing in the
world. And although diets have changed – they often include
nutrition and they're called detoxes, clean eating or reboots
now – come January 1st it can seem as if the world is following a regime of some kind. There's a global industry worth
billions devoted to ways of changing your body.[1] We're bom-
barded by images of perfection, by celebs extolling the virtues
of dubious laxative teas and dangerous Brazilian butt lifts.[2]

How has this impacted your attitude towards your body? If
someone asks you, 'Have you lost weight?' do you consider this
to be the highest of all praise? Do you sometimes wish for
plastic surgery? Thanks to the body positivity movement we're
becoming aware of these old patterns of unhelpful thinking.
But the huge shift that's needed, from body criticism to body
love, won't happen overnight. Many of us are still stuck with
the old programming; that we need to look a certain way in
order to be good enough. Despite 'knowing' it's all bullshit, we
still have to work hard to not want to jump on the bandwagon

when someone mentions the latest cosmetic procedure they've had or no-diet-diet (I mean, it's still a diet) that they're on.

Body shame is our default setting. Ever tried on eight different outfits and then declared you have 'nothing to wear!'? You're not alone. Body confidence issues affect the majority of us in some way or another. For years, I felt 'wrong' in my body, it didn't feel like my home, and I worried incessantly about its imperfections.

Here are some examples of what I and many others have experienced:

- Only having sex in pitch darkness because you can't bear the vulnerability of having your naked body on display.
- Staying away from dating because you can't understand how anyone could find you attractive.
- Cancelling a night out because your favourite top feels a little snugger than you'd like.
- Feeling so self-conscious and preoccupied about what you're wearing that you can't relax and enjoy a conversation with your close friends in a restaurant.
- Wasting hours beating yourself up about what you ate on holiday, leaving you feeling exhausted and withdrawn.

Deprogramming

We get a skewed idea of what a body should look like because of the messages we've been exposed to from an early age. We're so saturated with the media's idea of beauty that we've started to believe airbrushed perfection is 'normal' . . . and that makes 99.9 per cent of us abnormal. Essentially, we've been brainwashed, and it's messing with our confidence.

But it's absolutely possible to change this. Babies are not born with a hatred of their chubby thighs or Buddha bellies; it's something we learn later on. Start by telling yourself: this mental programme is way out of date and due for a change. Being brave means saying 'no thanks' to the ridiculous pressures we're subjected to and refusing to believe the media that tells us we're not enough. Michelle Elman, an author and body confidence coach, suggests that we question our thoughts and beliefs. 'Just because we think something doesn't mean it is true,' she told me. 'So many insecurities are fuelled by our thoughts but our thoughts are not fact. Just because you think you are ugly, or your thighs are ugly, doesn't mean it is true.'

To accept is best

For some people, loving their body can seem like too distant an aim to even try for. Acceptance or 'body neutrality' might be more realistic.

The way forward is to embrace yourself as you are. Even if you know deep down that your relationship with food or your lack of physical activity is unhealthy and you want it to change, know that change isn't going to happen by hating yourself. No one ever hated themselves healthy. Being mean to your body won't inspire and motivate you to take care of it. In fact, it'll do the exact opposite. Or you could have a 'healthy' body, but your mind will be messed up. There is nothing healthy about being 'skinny' or physically fit because you've punished yourself with a starvation diet or chained yourself to the treadmill for two hours a day. The healthiest and best way forward is to accept yourself exactly as you are, right now. From self-acceptance and love comes healthy change.

We've got it the wrong way around

My limbs work, so I'm not going to complain about
the way my body is shaped.
DREW BARRYMORE

Ask any person on the street, 'What makes someone attract-ive?' and nine times out of ten they will answer, 'Confidence.' Please don't let society's entirely fictional beauty standards stop you from feeling confident and knowing that you are attractive. Feel good in your skin now, because feeling beautiful is the most beautiful thing there is.

It's not something you decide once; it's a constant process of deciding again and again to accept yourself. This is how you build body acceptance and, after a while, confidence. We need to focus less on how we look and more on how we feel. What makes you feel good in your body? What makes your body feel good? What else is beautiful about you, aside from how you look?

This may sound like a silly example, but bear with me as the point it reveals isn't silly at all.

I used to have a real issue with (among other body parts) my feet. I disliked them for as long as I can remember. I have very high insteps – inherited from my dad – that give my feet an unusual S shape. My mum used to console me by saying they were like 'dancer's feet' (yeah, right).

Because I thought I was deformed, I've always kept my feet hidden. Then, ten years ago, I spent two weeks on a yoga course. I was not only barefoot for the duration but exposed to dozens of pairs of feet of all ages, shapes and sizes. There, I saw big feet, tiny feet, feet with huge bunions, flat feet, hairy toes, toe rings, webbed feet, veiny feet, tattooed feet and every-thing in between. I realized that my feet were normal in the continuum of types of feet – and all were perfectly fine.

What I want you to take away from this – right to the very heart of you – is that exactly the same is true for our whole bodies. There are endless variations of the human body, and yours is one of them. All of those variations are perfectly fine. However you feel about the various parts of your body, be assured that each one is worthy of acceptance.

What happens is, the world we see often does not reflect the beautiful diversity of the human body, in all its imperfection. Michelle Elman told me: 'Remove any content in your life that triggers comparison or makes you feel like your body is not good enough. Instead, fill your newsfeeds with a diverse group of people and, especially, people who look like you. It is a lot easier to see your own beauty, when you start surrounding yourself with more media that looks like you.' If your Instagram feed is made up of the perfectly rounded belfies (that's butt selfies, to you and me) of fitness influencers, of models with suspiciously plump lips and TV stars who are never 'grammed in the same outfit more than once, it's hard to know what 'real' looks like. And it's time to change what your mobile device is feeding you. It's time to seek out role models to follow that reflect the range of different people in our society and to read magazines that celebrate beauty of all kinds.

The boom in plastic surgery on the vulva is a case in point, as it has been fuelled by what people have seen on porn. If you're comparing your undercarriage to the surgically trimmed labia of porn stars, google diverse vulvas (or head to www.thevulvagallery.com) and realize that we are all different and all normal and all good enough. Beautiful does not have to look a 'certain' way.

What other ways can you open your mind to every expression of beauty that exists, not the one designed by an industry to sell you their products?

Let your body love what it loves

My all-time favourite poem is 'Wild Geese', by Mary Oliver, which really inspires me. It's a poem about not worrying about being good, or repenting, but being true to nature and following your heart.

If I find myself spiralling into self-criticism about my body, taking a cue from the poem, I remind myself that my body is a soft, sweet animal – like a cuddly dog or a lovable cat. I remember to treat and speak to my body with the same care and tenderness as I would a beloved pet. It's the most loving and loyal animal you will ever know. And it wants nothing else but to be your best friend. Your body is worthy of so much love.

To me this poem says, 'Be in your body, listen to it, love it, relax into it. You have nothing to be ashamed of.' Let your body want what it wants. That might be resting on the couch one day, and jogging around the park the next. It might mean savouring a cream scone today, and guzzling a green smoothie tomorrow. When we let go of the shame, blame and punishment of our bodies, we allow a natural equilibrium. And if you want to make changes in your health, they will come more easily when you're in a relaxed and accepting state.

Enjoy the ride

This is your one precious body. It isn't only a temple; it's a playground. So you may as well enjoy it. It's the vehicle through which you get to experience your life. Through it, you get to taste the first bite of a freshly baked Parisian croissant (or just one from Pret), hear the sound of your best mate laughing at one of your excellent jokes, feel your dog's heart beating as you snuggle up to her on the sofa, smell your newborn baby niece's head, and see the priceless look on your brother's face as you surprise him on his birthday. When you relax into your body and just enjoy it, your natural confidence will come through.

. . . .

Exercise: **Dear body; thank you, I love you.**

We need to flip our focus away from what we feel we lack and on to what we do have goin' on. Having gratitude for the things your body allows you to do and how it makes you feel is a powerful reminder of what truly matters. I love to do this practice as I get into bed each night. I think about five reasons why I'm grateful for my body that day, for what it helped me feel or do. I tell my body how much I love her. Over time this practice will rewire your brain to think of your body in a positive way. Here are some examples of what you might thank your body for.

Thank you to my round belly that gives my four-year-old such comfort when she snuggles up to me.

Thank you to my breasts that give me so much pleasure.

Thank you to my hands that let me stroke my partner's hair.

Thank you to my feet for letting me rock my four-inch heels.

Thank you to my nose that let me smell that stone-baked pizza.

. . . .

Exercise: **give yourself a massage**

This is great to do before or after a shower or bath. It's about getting away from what your body looks like and focusing on how it feels. Because it will feel good, both for the hand doing the touching and the part being touched. Close your eyes and give yourself a massage with some oil - coconut, almond, or even olive will do. Add in some essential oils to make it a multi-sensory experience. Focus on the feelings. Send love through your hands, imagining you're massaging your partner or your child if it helps you to be more loving.

• •

Exercise: get out of your head and into your body

We all know what it's like to be stuck in our heads. It can get very noisy in there – right?! It also takes us out of the moment, distracts us from what we really feel about a situation, what we really want to say or ask for. If we're more in our bodies, we're less likely to be worrying about what other people think of us and we're able to be present with what's happening. This exercise is adapted from one in Eckhart Tolle's *The Power of Now* and it's perfect for you if you're an overthinker who would like to be more present in their body.

Close your eyes and put your attention on your left arm. How do you know your left arm is there? What is it that you can feel? Perhaps you feel its temperature, the blood pumping or just an inner energy or vibration that's within your arm.

Now, keeping your eyes closed, spread that awareness to the other arm, your hands, your feet and legs, body, neck and head. You should now have an inner awareness of your own body. Congratulations! You're inhabiting your body now.

Can you keep that awareness, even if only for small moments, as you go about your day? Keep coming back to this awareness in your body whenever you remember – or set a reminder on your phone or calendar to do so.

Summary

★ Most of us have been brainwashed by diet culture.
★ Nobody has hated themselves healthy; accepting yourself is always the way forward.
★ Consume media and follow people who make you feel good about yourself.
★ Remind yourself of all the amazing things your body does for you.

PART SIX

How to stand up and be heard

CHAPTER 24

How to find your voice

The most courageous act is still to
think for yourself. Aloud.
COCO CHANEL

Do you struggle to speak up, to ask for what you want, to have a voice? There could be a million reasons why. Maybe your family were a particularly loud and vocal bunch and so, as a child, you couldn't get a word in. Or they were on the reserved side, so you learned to take more of a back seat and listen rather than speaking up. Perhaps, sadly, you were repeatedly told to shut up, to let the adults talk. Alternatively, not being able to find your voice could be about what's happening now. Perhaps you work in a male-dominated industry, or an office stuffed with extroverts, and speaking up makes you nervous. Or you harbour a belief that what you have to say isn't important.

While I was always loud with my family and people I knew well, I struggled to speak in groups. I would never put my hand up to ask a question in class at university and in my first job, I dreaded meetings where I was expected to contribute ideas – in fact, I was practically mute. I didn't believe I deserved the airtime, and was terrified of saying 'the wrong thing'. But things have changed so much for me, and it can for you too, I promise. You can find your voice. Whether you're softly spoken and want more gravitas, you're scared to speak up and share your opinions, or you tend to watch from the sidelines while other people do the talking, it is always possible to grow in confidence and learn to express yourself more.

Speaking out is a trait of a leader. Jessica Bennet, an editor for Sheryl Sandberg's non-profit, says while men are taught to lead, women are taught to nurture: 'So when women exhibit male traits – you know, decision-making, authority, leadership – we often dislike them, while men who exhibit those same traits are frequently deemed strong, masculine, and competent.'[1] Although things are changing, this male–female bias still exists. Add in our fear, self-doubt and self-sabotage, and why would we ever speak out? Part of the solution is to speak up anyway, to challenge these outdated notions, even if it means risking being disliked in the process. It means being brave enough to risk disapproval. And it means supporting other women when they speak up.

· ·

Exercise: your voice audit: where are you at?

Take some time to reflect on where you are when it comes to speaking up. And think about where you'd like to be, too. Sometimes the light of awareness is enough to kick-start the change you want. Write down the answers to these questions:

If you were 100 per cent confident, what would you say, and to whom?

When and where do you hold your tongue?

What frustrates you but you keep quiet about it?

If you knew you couldn't fail, how would you speak up and what would you say?

What would you love to say (or write), but haven't yet found the courage?

. . . .

The world needs your voice

A whopping 50 per cent of adults describe themselves as 'shy'. If you are one of them, it can be helpful to think: 'Half of the people I meet feel as uncomfortable as me.' Oh, and another crucial thing to remember is that just because someone shouts louder, it does *not* mean their viewpoint is more valid or more likely to be correct, although it's true that louder voices are more likely to be listened to and perceived as confident.

You need to know this: the world needs your unique perspective, your wisdom and your courage. Think of all the shy, quiet or introverted people who never get their ideas heard in the boardroom, or their stories told over the dinner table. Imagine all the creative ideas that never get expressed due to fear, the wisdom people keep to themselves because they don't believe what they have to say is of value, and the wrongs that can been righted if only we dare to speak up. If you don't express yourself fully, your knowledge and gifts won't get a chance to see the light of day, and as a result, everyone misses out.

I know how it feels to not want to speak up. When my sixth-form English teacher asked me a question in front of the class, I'd blush as red as a strawberry while reading the racier parts of Chaucer. I couldn't make eye contact with the teacher. I had problems speaking to people one on one, never mind in front of the class.

At university, studying nutrition, I had to present my projects to classmates, which I dreaded. Especially as, early in the course, one presentation ended up as an out-of-body experience – and not in a good way. As I stood up to speak, I felt all the blood drain from my face. A fuzzy, white mist descended in front of my eyes, my lungs felt on fire. Standing there in front of thirty classmates, I tried desperately to 'act normal', which only added to my inner panic. And then came one of the strangest and scariest feelings of my life; I felt as if I'd come out of my body and was floating a metre or so above myself, looking down. I later learned this is called 'dissociation', and it can happen when you're in a highly anxious state. The thought of it ever happening again left a cloud hanging over every other presentation.

Why shyness is still your ego in charge

I used to defend my shyness with a sort of pride. I was 'taking a back seat to let others shine', I was being 'selfless' by not claiming any attention, I was being 'modest' by being coy and reserved. The ego is your sense of self-importance and I believed that us shy people were somehow better because we had smaller egos (the irony is not lost on me). I thought putting other people first and listening rather than speaking were acts of kindness and even, gulp, signs of moral superiority.

What I have learned – and apologies if this truth bomb hits you a little hard, as it did me – is that shy people are the ones with the biggest egos. We take ourselves the most seriously. We want to be 'good' and 'liked' so much, we won't even attempt to speak up for fear of being criticized. We make ourselves inferior because we so badly want to be superior! As spiritual teacher and author Eckhart Tolle told Oprah, 'Deep down inside the shy person there's the unexpressed desire to be superior.' Discovering this has not only helped me to remember to take myself less seriously but also to remind myself, regularly, that there is nothing morally superior about hiding your light.

As a child, I loved to sing and would constantly sing around the house. Belinda Carlisle, Tina Turner, Fleetwood Mac, Destiny's Child . . . I'd sing my little heart out, hairbrush for a mic. I wasn't at all shy about singing. Honestly, I thought I was pretty good.

At the age of fifteen, I got my first acoustic guitar. I named him Greg and whipped him out at every opportunity. My friends were subjected to hours of five-chord wonders by Nirvana or Feeder, as we sat in the park, cans of cut-price cider in hand.

At the time, I'd just met my first boyfriend, Chris. One day, I can only imagine irritated by my insistence on hogging the guitar and playing the same chords repeatedly with my un-sophisticated strumming pattern, he snapped at me: 'You think you're so good at singing and playing the guitar. But you're not.'

My confidence shattered as my fragile ego took a massive hit. While I carried on playing my guitar in private, it would be another fifteen years until the next time I sang in public. What I told myself, for all those years, was that I was 'too shy' to sing. Even when, a few years ago, I tried to sing in front of my current boyfriend, who's literally never said one unkind word to me, I froze and the words wouldn't come out.

Then last summer, as part of my professional training, I attended a course on sound therapy. Sound therapy is about using sounds and vibrations from Tibetan bowls, gongs and your voice to relax and soothe the mind and body. Part of the course was about learning to free your voice, as so many people feel shy about the sound of their voice, and singing in particular. I confided in Michelle Avarard, the teacher, the whole sorry story of how my singing voice had ended up blocked. What she said to me echoed Eckhart Tolle: 'Shyness is actually when people have big egos, a big sense of self-importance. Our egos have a constant desire for validation, recognition, acceptance and approval. Shy people are afraid to shine because we're taking it all too personally and taking ourselves too seriously.'

What Michelle told me next really rang true; that we are all part of something much bigger, of nature and all of creation. As nature is just expressing itself through us, nothing we do is really about us – at all. Whether you're singing, reading a poem you wrote, acting on a stage or pitching an idea to a client, expressing your gifts and sharing your inspiration, creativity or experience can never be wrong. Since that day, instead of asking myself, 'Who am I to speak up?' I ask, '*Who am I to keep this to myself?*' I also realized, whether I'm a good singer or not is no big deal.

That night, there was an open mic performance. Despite the pep talk from Michelle, I decided not to take part. As I slunk back to my room, I felt a huge wave of disappointment with myself. I sat, slumped on the bed, acutely aware of my guitar resting idly in the corner.

I have found, when it comes to taking action that's a little bit brave, there is often a crunch point, when you have to make a choice. This one stretched out from seconds into minutes, as I wavered. Could I face my terror of being heard? Or should I stay safely in my room? Then, at the last minute, I heard a voice in my head ask, 'What do I need to do to overcome this fear?' My heart answered immediately, 'You need to go and do it'.

I grabbed my guitar and headed to the room where the

performance was taking place. When it was my turn to sing, I could feel my pulse beating through my whole body, the adrenaline pounding through me. I took a deep breath and I began. I was very far from perfect; my voice cracked, I messed up a few words. But I did it.

Afterwards, it felt simultaneously hugely momentous but also like no big deal. Once I'd done it, I wondered, 'What was all the fuss about?!' But I also knew it was a big step in expressing myself more freely. I had busted through the blockage that had kept me stuck; I felt a surge of confidence, more capable than ever before.

What I discovered was, overcoming my fear of singing was about having the courage to be average, to be imperfect or even to be rubbish, especially at first. I needed to remember that we are all an expression of nature, that it's not really about us. Confidence, it turns out, is 'knowing you are not that big of a deal', as Marianne Williamson has put it; it's about taking yourself less seriously. My voice cracked in front of thirty people – and it didn't matter one bit. Knowing you can falter – and survive – is an important part of becoming more self-assured. After all, if you can do that, you literally have nothing to lose.

It's not really about you

Whether you're sharing your ideas in a business meeting, giving a speech at your best friend's wedding or performing a song you wrote, none of it is about you. This is true of any words, music, information, wisdom, jokes. It all already exists, out in the world; there are no new ideas. It doesn't define you, it's just moving through you. It is life expressing itself, through you, and your job is to let it flow.

We often have fear of success and of failure simultaneously. We might be scared that what we have to say is bad or wrong, but also that it might be really good, bring us more attention, make us feel embarrassed or mean we're asked to do more work. And moreover, we may be scared that if we do eventually fail after success, we'll fall from an even greater height.

Your first step is simply to take some action, one tiny move towards the scary thing; going to an event solo, putting your hand up to ask a question in a workshop, or standing up to your colleague who's a bully. Take that step and you'll soon learn you can handle anything that comes up as a result. Have the courage to risk being imperfect and you'll feel your confidence grow.

The secret to confidence

OK, OK, there is no ultimate secret. But if there was, it would be this: people who are naturally confident are not necessarily so because they think they're amazing, have extensively pondered their own brilliance and have said 4,000 positive affirmations in the mirror that day. No. In fact, you might be surprised to hear, confident people don't really think about themselves at all.

Thinking about ourselves too much is what causes us to get nervous and fearful about speaking up. Naturally confident women, on the other hand, are present, aware, focused completely on what they're doing, saying and hearing. They're in the moment, letting life and their own wisdom express itself through them. They give things a try without too much overthinking.

Next time you're faced with a confidence-testing situation, get yourself into the moment. Focus intently on your surroundings. Notice the scenery, the people, the smells and the feeling of your feet on the ground. Deepen your breath and feel your belly rise and fall. Direct your attention outwards on to what you're doing, towards the person or people you're speaking to. Doing this will instantly distract you from your thoughts.

Between the testing times, it's worth trying mindfulness meditation. This is a great way to strengthen your ability to be present, to learn how to focus on what's happening rather than on your interior life. Apps such as Headspace or Buddhify make the process easy; you'll find doing just ten minutes a day will give you a great start.

Summary

★ The world needs your voice and your ideas; please don't keep them to yourself.
★ Whether you're speaking in public, singing or telling a story at the table, it's never really about you; life is expressing itself through you.
★ Confident people think about themselves less and are focused on the present moment.

CHAPTER 25

Retrain your brain

Being brave doesn't have to mean taking massive, terrifying action – I mentioned the concept of micro-bravery in an earlier chapter. At the same time, it's not bravery unless it's a bit of a challenge.

In coaching, we use a model from Karl Rohnke called Comfort, Stretch, Panic. The idea is, you need to move out of your comfort zone and into the stretch zone – but stop before you reach the panic zone.

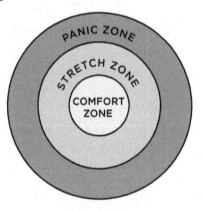

The first time you move out of your comfort zone, you'll find it hard. But after a while, it will stop being uncomfortable and become your new normal. This is your comfort zone expanding. Next, take another step out of your comfort zone, to stretch yourself again. Each time you do this, think of it as sharpening your sword, allowing you to slay even bigger, scarier future dragons.

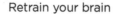

Exercise: **work out your zones**

Draw three circles on a piece of paper. Label the inner circle 'comfort zone', the next circle 'stretch zone' and the outer one 'panic zone'.

Step 1: In the inner circle, make a list of the actions you feel comfortable with. Examples might be: socializing with my close friends, making phone calls at work, meeting people one on one.

Step 2: For the next circle, ask yourself, what would be a stretch for me? That is, not so it feels impossible or your palms sweat at the mere thought, but enough to feel slightly uncomfortable. Examples of this might be: socializing with people I've just met, being on a conference call at work, meeting with people in a group larger than two.

Step 3: For the outer circle, think about what fills you with panic. Maybe it's the thought of chairing a meeting or going to a networking event? If so, in they go. This circle is to be addressed at a later date.

Step 4: Now, what action can you take, today, to move into your stretch zone?

Tell your brain everything is OK

Our old friend fear is often the biggest barrier between us and feeling more confident. But we can retrain our brains to expect a situation to be safe, and even to go well.

Fear comes from a part of the brain called the amygdala. It's nicknamed our 'lizard' or 'reptilian' brain, because it's the oldest part of the brain, in charge of fight or flight and the other survival responses that evolved to keep us safe.

. . . .

Exercise: how to train your lizard brain

If fear is what's preventing you from speaking up, this exercise will retrain your nervous system into responding without it. The method – known as 'classical conditioning' – is similar to the famous psychological experiment, nicknamed 'Pavlov's dogs', where dogs were trained to salivate in response to a particular sound. The experiment began with the dogs hearing the tick of a metronome, then being fed. After a few repetitions, the dogs began to salivate, anticipating food, every time they heard the tick. Now, you are going to do some conditioning on your brain. Follow these steps:

Step 1: Go into a situation that is in your stretch zone (look back at the previous exercise where you worked out your zones).

Step 2: Don't die.

Step 3: Your brain learns that you don't die, and in fact, it's safe to speak up.

Step 4: Rinse and repeat.

Step 5: Celebrate how amazing you are.

. . . .

Your lizard brain will learn through experience that speaking up is safe. It will learn you're capable. It will learn, even if things do go marginally tits up, you didn't die and it's less of a big deal than you'd thought. If you do get embarrassed, or lose your train of thought, even better. Because your brain will learn you didn't die then, either!

Eventually, just as Pavlov's dogs associated food with the ticking sound, your lizard will come to associate speaking up or going out of your comfort zone with positive results. These could be, for example, a sense of achievement, a pay rise or adoring fans (or at the very least a bit of praise from your colleagues). Your lizard will realize there is no threat to your survival. It will call off the alarm and stand down.

Remember, don't wait for confidence to land in your lap (because it won't). Confidence comes from taking brave action. Fear shrinks when you walk towards it, so start planning what you'll do. It could be speaking up to say no, making a request for what you want or calling out an injustice. It's time to act.

Know fear is normal

When I hear talk about 'fear-less' women, I feel perplexed. Only psychopaths and dead people feel no fear. For the rest of us, with emotions and a pulse, fear is a normal, natural part of life.

Rather than try to stamp out our fear, we need to embrace it. I can promise you that 99 per cent of women (the other 1 per cent are the psychopaths!) feel afraid every now and again. Many of us feel afraid a lot, in fact, every time we act outside of what we normally do. But when we accept fear as human and natural, then push through and take action anyway, we will discover a sense of bravery and confidence at the other end.

Move up the ladder of bravery

Remember, you are a brave warrior woman and are capable of doing anything you set your heart on. All you have to do is keep moving, inch by inch, up the ladder of bravery towards your end goal of confidence in every situation (or at the very least, feeling more able to do things you couldn't do before).

In fact, in any area where fear holds you back, you can create a ladder of bravery. The ladder shows you the manageable steps you can take towards ultimate bravery – starting with the easiest. This example, below, about speaking in public, is from my own life. By climbing the ladder, I went from feeling pretty awkward and uncomfortable in even one-on-one situations to being able to speak in front of a crowd of hundreds and go on live radio. And one day, when I get my chance to go on live TV, I'll grab it with both hands.

HARDEST

Being interviewed
on live TV

Singing in front
of others

Being interviewed
on live radio

Speaking at Stylist
Live to 200 people

Delivering training
for businesses

Running workshops
for 30 people

Networking events

One-on-one
meetings

EASIEST

. . . .

Exercise: draw your own ladder of bravery

Think of an area where fear holds you back. In which situations would you love to speak up? Which would be the easiest, and which the most challenging? Make a list, ordering it from easiest to hardest, with the easiest at the bottom. What action can you take today (like, right now) to make a start on the first rung? Make a commitment by scheduling something into your diary, telling a friend or making a phone call.

. . . .

Remember to be kind

Compassion for yourself is key when it comes to moving out of your comfort zone. Having the courage just to give things a go is an act worthy of your kindness. Think of how you'd speak to a child who was scared but willing to give it a try; you'd be kind, gentle, loving and encouraging. We need to be the same way with ourselves. We all instinctively know that scolding the child or telling her she's an idiot wouldn't work in helping her to improve. So why do it to yourself?

Challenges to find your voice

Here are suggestions for some challenges that will help you move out of your comfort zone and into your stretch zone (you may find some harder than others!):

- Sing a song at your local open mic night.
- Read a poem you wrote to your friends.

- Ask someone at the gym how many sets they have left to do on the squat rack.
- Ask for directions.
- At a restaurant, ask for a dish which isn't on the menu.
- Tell a story loudly and clearly to a group of friends around the dinner table.
- At a conference, introduce yourself to three new people.
- When a piece of work is challenging in your new job, ask for help.

Summary

- ★ You can retrain your brain, like training a dog, to forget fear and expect things to go well.
- ★ Fear is normal, everyone experiences it.
- ★ Challenge yourself step by step, and move up the ladder of bravery.

CHAPTER 26

Find the courage to be criticized

*People will love you. People will hate you. And none
of it will have anything to do with you.*

ABRAHAM HICKS

Never, in the history of womankind, has anyone been univer-
sally liked. Someone, somewhere probably thought Mother
Teresa was a bit OTT. Some folks don't care that much for
Ellen. Some, probably, think Beyoncé is annoying AF. But if
these women had ignored their purpose or watered down their
personalities in order to be liked by a few more people, the
world would be a far worse place. Part of true confidence is
finding the courage to be disliked.

Before speaking on stage to over 200 people, I remember
frantically telling my boyfriend Aidan of my hopes for the
talk. 'I want everyone to enjoy it. Everyone needs to laugh at
this bit! And I want all of them to leave feeling inspired!'

I was searching for reassurance, but instead, with his usual
Sagittarian frankness, he served up a healthy dose of realism.
'Not everyone is going to like it. And that's OK.'

I let what he said sink in. And it dawned on me: my inner
control freak was labouring under the assumption I could create the 'perfect' talk, one every single person in the audience
would love. But this is impossible. Despite our best attempts
to gain approval, ultimately what people think of us is *out of
our control.*

There are endless reasons why someone might dislike what you have to say. It could conflict with their personal experience. It may hit a nerve that you couldn't even know exists. You might remind them of someone they don't like. Your voice could grate on their nerves. They may not gel with your vibe. They might be jealous or find you threatening. Or they may simply not like the look of you. All of this is outside of your control. And all of this is A-OK.

When I let go of trying to please everyone and be perfect, I found I could breathe easy and focus on doing the best talk that I knew how.

Being OK with the possibility of not being liked is the key to your freedom and peace of mind. Remember, you don't like everyone the same amount. We all have preferences. This doesn't mean the people you don't like are worth any less than you – we are all equal at the end of the day. They might just not be your cup of tea.

Warmth and strength: a winning combo

Until fairly recently, it was assumed women who wanted to get ahead at work needed to act like men. Especially in male-dominated corporate industries. Women thought they needed to take on the dominant macho values to get the big jobs. But do we really need to act like ball breakers to get ahead? It seems not. Numerous reports suggest when women 'try to act like men', not being themselves or acting aggressively, they are disliked for it. Social psychologist Amy Cuddy and fellow researchers, writing in the *Harvard Business Review* suggest that the best strategy is to first connect, then lead.[1] Their research shows the traditionally more 'feminine' qualities of warmth and connection, rather than 'masculine' authority and aggression, can be an asset, not a hindrance, when it comes to being heard.

Connecting first, building trust and showing warmth, puts us in the best position to lead and influence others. 'Warmth is the conduit of influence: it facilitates trust and the communication and absorption of ideas,' writes Cuddy. When we combine warmth with strength, it's a winning combination. Far from needing to be aggressive to gain respect and be listened to, being our warm, friendly selves works better.

Tall poppy syndrome

> You cannot easily fit women into a structure
> that is already coded as male; you have
> to change the structure.
> **MARY BEARD, *WOMEN & POWER: A MANIFESTO***

The Australian term 'tall poppy syndrome' refers to those deemed a little too successful, confident or prominent, who therefore need to be 'cut down to size'. We've all seen it happen to celebrities by the press. Taylor Swift and Anne Hathaway, for example, were at first loved by the media, then later torn down. Maybe you've seen it happen in real life to a friend? Perhaps you've even been the one to bad-mouth another, purely for the fact they're doing well and you felt the need to knock them off their throne. Tall poppy syndrome most definitely exists in the UK, where we love the underdog but also love to hate the person considered to have been on top for too long.

But who decides why or when someone gets cut down? Our society is rife with double standards towards women, less so towards men. Women get body shamed for being too thin, or too curvy. You can be cut down for trying hard with your appearance or for not seeming to try hard enough. Or for being too sexy or not sexy enough, too confident or not confident enough. We're either too passive or we're selfish and aggressive. There are so many ways we can be judged and found to be failing a seemingly random code of conduct or set of expectations.

Knowing that, do we keep ourselves small, our heads down and our voices quiet? Or do we risk speaking up, being proud, assertive and confident . . . and potentially being criticized or chopped down to size for it?

While we cannot change the culture overnight, we can start by changing our own mindset. The question is: are you going to let the fact that someone else feels jealous or threatened stop you from feeling confident or taking action? Are you going to let what someone else might think stop you from living the best life that you can? Will you join me in refusing to participate in this, and instead, lift up other women rather than tearing them down?

As you grow in confidence, there will be people who feel threatened, but there will be others for whom you become an inspiration. I recently saw an American woman, in a similar industry to me, boldly and proudly selling her services and talking about the incredible benefits people could get from working with her. The old me would have thought, 'Wow, she's so arrogant, who does she think she is?!' But I now know, the reason for my past bitchiness was because I'd repressed and denied the part of me that wanted to be as bold. So instead, I allowed myself to feel inspired by her, to use her confidence to give myself permission to be bolder and more confident in my own work.

. . . .

Exercise: **find the courage to be a tall poppy**

Ask yourself the following questions:

In what ways could you speak up and encourage others to do the same?

How could your bravery help others to conjure up their own courage?

How can you allow yourself to be inspired, rather than threatened, by other confident women?

If you're looking for permission to do any of the things you think of, permission granted! Remember that if you're critical of a confident or successful women, it could be that you're suppressing the part of you that is (or wants to be) confident and successful too.

Summary

★ It is impossible to be liked by everyone –
and that's OK.
★ Let's support other women who are doing well
rather than cutting them down to size.

CHAPTER 27

Why role models matter

We have all learned by copying others; walking, talking and feeding ourselves, to name just a few examples. The reason we're able to learn this way is because we have brain cells called mirror neurons. These specialized nerve cells were discovered by accident in the 1980s by neuroscientist Giacomo Rizzolatti and his colleagues.[1] Studying the brains of monkeys, they happened to notice that the same neurons fired when the monkeys watched the researchers do an action, for example picking up a peanut, as when the monkey itself picked up a peanut.

Want to know why men automatically wince and cover their genitals when they see someone on TV getting kicked in the nuts (ouch!)? Mirror neurons. Their existence also explains why we salivate when we watch a slo-mo video of a knife cutting into a gooey chocolate fondant #foodporn. It's because the same part of your brain is firing up, as if you were about to eat the dessert too.

Mirroring someone is part of the process of natural learning. As we watch the people we admire, our brains are practising what they do. If you take note of what it is that makes that person so impressive, even better. Whether you observe a colleague who's killing it in the boardroom, watch TED talks of your favourite speakers, notice how your sister assertively stands up to your mum, or head out to watch your favourite beat poet live, watch what they do and how they do it.

The principle of NLP modelling

The founders of NLP (Neuro-Linguistic Programming), Richard Bandler and John Grinder, proposed that the best way to become good at something was to learn from other people who were doing it well. Modelling involves learning from a successful person, making their qualities your own. It isn't about impersonating or trying to act like them – that would not be cool or clever – but rather learning their processes, their abilities, skills and attitudes so you can use them to your advantage.

Who is your role model? Who has the sort of bravery, confidence or assertiveness you really admire? It could be a celeb, a work colleague, a goddess from mythology, a tutor at university or a friend. Some of my favourite inspirational women are:

- Serena Williams
- Lena Dunham
- Moana
- Amal Clooney
- Malala Yousafzai
- Oprah Winfrey
- Daenerys Targaryen
- Emma Watson

. . . .

Exercise: watch a video of your role model

Notice everything about them, the way they hold themselves, the way they move, where they look. Make a note of the way they speak, breathe, the pauses they take, the language they use. What is their attitude? How do they respond?

Make a note of the following to refer back to for the visualization in the next exercise.

What do you think they believe about them-selves? What have they said about their beliefs?

For example: 'What I have to say is useful.' 'I am more than good enough.' 'I am smart, strong and lovable.'

What do you think they are telling themselves? What is their internal dialogue likely to be?

For example: 'I've got this! I am in my element! I love speaking to people!'

What is their posture? How do they move? What gestures do they make?

For example: relaxed, open body language, confident hand gestures, slow movements.

How do they speak? What is their tone? Do they speak fast or slow?

For example: pausing often or not at all, taking deep breaths.

What do you imagine it feels like to be in their body in that moment, looking so calm and confident? Can you sense their energy?

For example: expansive, grounded.

• •

Exercise: **step into your role model's shoes meditation**

You've watched a video of your role model and made detailed notes of what inspires you about them. Now download this meditation in the bonuses at www.calmer-you.com/brave-bonus.

Get comfortable and close your eyes. Take some deep breaths and imagine your body relaxing more with every out breath.

Now imagine your role model is standing in front of you. Notice what it is about her, what she does and how she does it, that you'd love to learn from and make your own. Notice the way she moves and holds herself.

Now step into her shoes and feel what it feels like to be in her body. Notice the feeling of holding yourself the way she does. Notice the posture. Feel the confident, positive energy.

Imagine speaking up with the same self-assurance as she does. Feel the sense of self-belief. Notice the positive, confident thoughts. Hear your voice as calm, clear and articulate. Really feel as though you are experiencing speaking up from this person's perspective.

Imagine your unconscious mind downloading this way of being and making it your own. Then step out of her shoes and take on board this new internal image of yourself as this confident, assertive person.

. . . .

Channel your role model

As an alternative to the meditation exercise, you can simply go into situations and channel your role model's energy.

When I need extra strength, I channel my nana, Agatha. Agatha was a strong and resilient person who Dad described as a 'rock'. She had a difficult time of things; she lost her older son, and her husband died of cancer in his forties. But I remember her as always calm and incredibly loving. Plus she had an amazing career making beautiful clothes for the Queen.

When I need an extra boost of inner stability, resilience and calm, I channel her, imagining her strength being inside me too (and after all, I do have some of her DNA).

Summary

★ We learn by watching others. We can use confident people as our role model to help us to be more confident too.

★ Who is your role model? How can you gain inspiration from them and learn from them?

CHAPTER 28

How to speak in public

I'm all too familiar with feeling nervous for weeks before a speaking engagement. I remember having hideous dread hanging over me along with some seriously irrational thoughts and feelings. It sounds dramatic, but part of me used to wonder if I'd make it back from the talk; it seemed impossible to imagine a time when the talk would be over.

These days, I still get a tickle of nerves before I speak, which is totally normal, but it no longer stops me from agreeing to speak. I've actually come to, dare I say it, enjoy public speaking. There's always something a bit scary about putting yourself and your ideas out there, but there's something a bit magical about it, too. When you're speaking, you have an opportunity to educate, inspire, reassure or give important information to the audience. You don't know all the ways you might be helping someone.

It's often reported that public speaking is our biggest fear, over and above our fear of death, so it's in no way a small challenge. Give yourself permission to feel what you feel and instead of fighting against your nerves, go with it. There is a lot to be said for accepting it's OK to feel nervous. Surf the waves of anxiety, knowing the sea will be calm again soon.

Nine techniques for public speaking

Some nerves beforehand are normal – it would be weird if you had no feelings. But obviously you don't want fear to keep you at home, quivering under the bedcovers. These nine techniques will turn self-doubt into self-confidence and help you overcome your fear of public speaking, whether it's to an audience of one or of one thousand.

1. Get excited

In a study at Harvard Business School, participants were asked to bust out the eighties banger 'Don't Stop Believin'' by Journey, on stage in front of their peers. Researchers found singers performed better when they labelled their nervous feelings as excitement, rather than trying to calm themselves down.[1] Simply say out loud to yourself, 'I'm excited.' Or write yourself a little message saying, 'Get excited!' This will shift your perspective so you view the situation as an opportunity rather than a threat. You can also tell yourself that a little bit of nervous energy will fuel your performance, helping you embrace the experience rather than fighting against it.

2. Know the room

Knowing the environment you're going to be speaking in will help put your mind at ease. If it's possible, do a recce of the room, so you can get to know it. Stand on the stage or at the table where you're going to be speaking. You could do a dress rehearsal of your speech too. Along similar lines, as people come into the room, before you start your talk or speech, introduce yourself to a few of them. Getting to know people, even briefly, will mean you'll see more friendly faces as you look out at your audience.

3. Breathe deeply

A long, deep exhale activates the parasympathetic nervous system, also called the rest-and-digest system. This is the primal part of your brain and body that kicks in when there's no danger around. To turn on its calming effect, simply lengthen your out breath. Before you step up to the podium, or before it's your turn to introduce yourself around the table, take some deep, belly breaths. Make the out breath slightly longer than the in breath; I suggest you count to three for your inhale and five to exhale.

4. Practise, practise, practise

Nothing will make you feel more nervous than being under-prepared. As you get more experienced at speaking, you'll learn to trust in your ability to think on your feet and find the right words. You'll develop the confidence to find your flow. But until then, practice is the most helpful component in ensuring you feel self-assured. Practise in the mirror and to a friend or a trusted colleague. Being certain you know your stuff will build your confidence – and before long, you'll be able to speak off the cuff, too.

5. Listen back

Now this might sound incredibly daunting: film yourself or record your voice, then watch or listen back to it. Nobody likes the sound of their own voice (well, OK, some people do!). Yes, your voice will sound weird . . . to you. Yes, you'll think,

'Is that what I sound like?! Argh!' There is a reason for this; on a recording, you are hearing your voice with just your eardrums instead of also hearing it conducted through your skull and jaw bones.

Recording yourself will give you such useful insight. When I first started The Calmer You Podcast, I could not believe how often I said the word 'and' when it wasn't needed, and the phrase 'you know' when I was thinking of what to say next. Once I knew, I could stop. Though you may find it cringeworthy to hear yourself back, if you don't know you constantly say 'um' how will you ever be able to change? Be brave and record yourself speaking. You soon get used to it, I promise. Knowledge is power!

6. Move up the ladder of bravery

If you've got a big challenge coming up, maybe giving a speech at your best mate's wedding or a work function, work up to it slowly. Start with a small test such as raising your hand to ask a question in a meeting, asking for help in a clothes shop or telling a story during a big family dinner. Now, think about what the next challenge could be, the next step up the ladder of public speaking bravery. Working up to the big one, step by step, each bold act will desensitize you to fear, allowing your confidence to build slowly.

7. Turn up the dial

Think of all your years of experience, all the education you've had to get you to where you are today, all the valuable skills and abilities you have learned. Now imagine that within you there is a dial controlling your level of confidence. Imagine turning it up and, as you do, feel every cell, muscle and fibre of your body being infused with confidence and self-assurance. To supercharge your confidence, imagine doing this on the train ride to work before your talk, or before you get out of bed in the morning.

8. Slow right down

When I started working with clients one on one for public speaking, I discovered speed is an issue every ... single ... time. We speak too fast, sometimes with machine-gun speed, because we don't believe we deserve the airtime and we want to make it be over as quickly as possible. However, with more speed comes less precision; we're more likely to muddle our words or lose our train of thought. And it's hard for the audience to absorb what's being said when it's presented too fast. Practise speaking slowly and leaving appropriate pauses. These might be longer than you'd think. Slowing down gives you more impact and gravitas, allows for what you've said to land and be absorbed. Taking a few deep breaths before you start and a single deep breath between each section of your talk will create a pause and help you slow down.

9. Visualization

Mental rehearsal is a technique used by athletes before big competitions and by top public speakers. It involves visualizing the event beforehand in great detail, and imagining it going well. When we vividly imagine in this way, the same areas of the brain are activated as if we were doing it for real. It trains your brain to feel prepared.

. . . .

Exercise: **visualization**

Start with this simple visualization. You can do this at home – all you need is a quiet space where you won't be disturbed.

Close your eyes and relax. Take some deep breaths and allow yourself to settle a little more comfortably into your seat.

Now use all of your senses to play a movie in your mind of you, feeling poised and at ease, exuding self-assurance, making eye contact and pausing when needed, speaking clearly and slowly. Imagine your upright posture, your feeling of excitement and how much you are enjoying saying what you want to say.

This detailed mental rehearsal will help you face your next public speaking opportunity with increased confidence, preparing you for success.

Summary

★ Public speaking is something many people dislike but it's a skill you can develop – and learn to enjoy.
★ Practise: challenge yourself and remember to slow down and breathe deeply.

CHAPTER 29

Learn the art of communication

Clients often come to me with specific issues around speaking in public. Whether you want to own the room like Oprah or be calmer like Michelle Obama, I've included some key issues that come up time and time again, such as being interrupted and learning to give feedback. Remember, these skills aren't just for work situations, they are key in your personal life too.

This advice will show you how to make maximum impact with what you're saying and how to communicate clearly and gracefully.

The art of interrupting

It's rude to interrupt, right? That's what was drummed into us from an early age. And although it can be rude, it may also, at times, be necessary.

If you're concerned you won't get your chance to speak, or if you're aware that what the speaker is saying isn't as valuable as what you have to say, chip in when the speaker pauses to take a breath. Don't qualify what you're saying with 'sorry', 'maybe', 'just' or 'I could be wrong but'. This language will project an image of self-doubt and you don't want that. You might find it useful to start what you say with one of these phrases:

- 'Can I stop you there?'
- 'I just want to pause you there for a minute.'
- 'And just to add to that . . .'

How to avoid being interrupted

No one will ever forget the moment Taylor Swift's acceptance speech was interrupted by Kanye West at the 2009 MTV Video Music Awards. He even took her microphone out of her hands. Would he have done that if she was male? The science backs up what many women report: people interrupt women more than they do other men.[1]

Kieran Snyder, an empirical linguist, conducted an observational study in her workplace at a tech company.[2] She observed 900 minutes of meetings and found men were three times more likely to interrupt women than they were other men. Even women were more likely to interrupt women than men, accounting for 85 per cent of their interruptions. The results may in part be due to the fact that people with more power are more likely to interrupt (and men tend to hold more positions of power). The fact remains, being stopped mid-flow is more likely if you're a woman, and it can be confidence crushing. It can also be frustrating, especially when you have something important to say or you're trying to make your mark.

You do have options for avoiding being interrupted. You can just carry on speaking over the interrupter, possibly getting louder. You can say to them 'I'd like to finish what I was saying' or 'one moment' (perhaps while holding up a finger) before finishing your point. The feminist journalist Helen Lewis, author of *Difficult Women: A History of Feminism in 9 Fights*, told me: '[Sometimes it's about] just plowing on and refusing the interruption. Or stating what you want to say again. If you are being interrupted a lot in an aggressive way there is a great power in noticing it and saying, "Can I just get to the end of this sentence please?".'

In 2016, the *Washington Post* reported that female staff working in the dog-eat-dog atmosphere of the White House had come up with a strategy called 'amplification' to support each other in meetings.[3] This involved women repeating each other's points, each time giving the original speaker the credit for their idea. This is something we can all do too; support the key points other women make, making sure everyone is aware of where the good ideas have come from.

Use confident body language

You can send a signal to others using confident body language that you're not to be interrupted. Stand or sit up straight, turn your body towards the person who's speaking, keep your arms open instead of crossed and make eye contact. Make sure your hands are visible as hiding them under the table or behind your back can make you look nervous or uncomfortable. You can either gesture or rest them on the table. Evidence also suggests that both smiling and leaning back when at a boardroom table could increase your chances of being interrupted.[4] So be sure to lean in.

Avoid 'upspeak'

Those of us who grew up with a lot of *Sweet Valley High* and *Home and Away* – or any American or Aussie TV series – may have adopted this habit of raising the pitch of our voices at the end of a sentence. But did you know that it undermines the confidence others have in us? 'Upspeak' aka 'Going up? At the end of a sentence?' makes every sentence you say sound like a question and can, therefore, make you sound less credible, as if you're second-guessing yourself. And it's a speaking tic that's most commonly heard amongst young women. While I'm not suggesting you should change your voice or put on a fake voice, it's good to be aware if you tend to upspeak, so that in important situations you can speak with more assurance.

Don't try 'vocal fry'

Or 'Kardashian-speak', as I like to call it. You'll know it when you hear it; it's when we drop our voices very low and the words sound drawn-out and creaky, as though they're coming from the back of the throat. A study of young women found that vocal fry made them appear less competent and hirable.[5] Yes, you might have caught vocal fry from OD'ing on *KUWTK* (no judgement here!) but you can change. If you suspect you're doing it, record a clip of yourself speaking and listen back to it. And if you are, Allison Shapira, CEO of Global Public Speaking LLC, says here's how to stop: take a deep breath, then speak on the out breath, letting the breath carry your voice.[6] So, the next time you introduce yourself, do as Allison says: 'Imagine speaking on the breath so that you support the words and don't let them drop into your throat.' The result will be a louder, more resonant and more self-assured and powerful sound.

How to speak up and give feedback

Giving feedback can be incredibly tough. We don't want to offend people, we want them to like us. We may be afraid of their reaction if they don't take our criticism well. It may feel more comfortable to keep quiet and put up with whatever is going on.

However, have you considered that keeping quiet could actually be doing the other person a disservice? If they're unaware of what they're doing wrong, how can they improve? If you end up breaking up with a friend because there's something they keep doing but you don't have the courage to tell them about, you'll leave them wondering what happened, perhaps going on to repeat it in the future. It's easy to get into the habit of speaking badly about people behind their backs, instead of telling them the truth to their face. But you don't have to risk your relationship by speaking out.

Examples might be:

- Letting your partner know you're not in love with *that thing* they do in the bedroom.
- Telling your best friend you feel hurt when she takes weeks to get back to you.
- Expressing your thoughts calmly, clearly and assertively to an employee who consistently comes in late.

Try to be kind

There are kind, constructive ways to give feedback that will meet your needs and give the other person the opportunity to learn and grow.

- Following the principles of non-violent communication is a gentle and easy way to give feedback – more on this in Chapter 34 'How to communicate your needs'.
- Focus on the behaviour, not the person. So instead of saying, 'You're so disorganized!' say,

'I notice your work is quite disorganized.' Instead of telling them, 'You're a bad friend!' say, 'I've noticed you haven't replied to my messages recently.'
- Acknowledge what they're doing well and give praise for that, alongside the feedback.
- Be specific and use examples in your comments, rather than making vague assertions. On which days was your employee late? In what exact way do you feel your friend is taking advantage of you?

Use a coaching style

Coaching is all about asking the right questions and, in doing so, promoting the other person's awareness and sense of responsibility so they want to make the change needed. This sort of feedback works best in the workplace, when you are managing someone else.

In the classic coaching book *Coaching for Performance*, Sir John Whitmore suggests questions that will promote awareness and responsibility in the other person. Examples might be:

- 'What are you most pleased with?'
- 'What would you do differently?'
- 'What are you learning?'

If you get stuck, remember you can ask for help and advice from someone higher up than you at work, or ask to go on a training course.

How to receive feedback

Do what you feel in your heart to be right –
for you'll be criticized anyway.
ELEANOR ROOSEVELT

So you made a mistake or you didn't do the right thing? As human beings, we have a tendency to generalize and catastrophize, but just because you did one thing wrong, it doesn't mean you as a person are a complete disaster (although if you're anything like me, I know your mind has been there). One mistake doesn't define you. Neither does the fact you may not have picked up a skill you need at work, or there's one you need to improve.

Tara Mohr, author and coach, says, 'Look at praise and criticism as information about the people giving it.' It's about their likes and dislikes, their preferences and their experience of the world. And as I said before, it's OK not to be liked by everyone. If it's at work, the purpose is to get better. If it's a personal relationship, the purpose should be to improve that relationship. Either way, there's a good reason behind it.

Receiving a lot of criticism as a child can lead to shame or to the child growing up being overly self-critical because we didn't have the ability to rationalize it then. This is true for Kayla, twenty-eight. 'My dad was extremely critical of me growing up, about everything from my school performance, my choice in friends, my preferences and opinions to the way I walked. So as an adult, I'm super sensitive to criticism and, unless it's delivered in an obviously gentle way, I am easily hurt and upset. But I'm working on this.'

What Kayla is learning as an adult, and you can too, is that when criticism is constructive, it can be useful.

Six steps to receiving criticism

Any criticism can be painful and hard to hear but the good news is, the more you receive, the easier it gets. You grow a thicker skin. And as you learn you can handle it, your resilience increases.

1. Listen with openness

Allow yourself to really hear what the other person is saying. Author and teacher Byron Katie asks us to question ourselves: 'Can I go there?' What she means is, can you go to the place where that criticism is true and see where the other person is coming from? Can you go to the place where you *are* lazy, disorganized or selfish, and see it from their perspective? Being able to see the other person's point of view and having acceptance of ourselves for our faults, allows us to relax into the criticism more easily. It may still hurt, but if we find that we can hold on, hear the other person out without getting defensive, we give ourselves the best chance of being able to use the information constructively.

2. Breathe before you respond

When we feel under attack, it's a natural human response to go into defensive mode. When we react emotionally or when we're afraid, blood flow goes towards the emotional, fear centre of the brain, the amygdala, and away from the frontal cortex, the rational part. We can't think clearly. That's when you find yourself scrambling for an excuse, shutting down or going into counter-attack. At this point, it's important to breathe deeply and wait for as long as it takes to get calm, before you respond. When a critical email hits your inbox, wait an hour before replying, to give yourself some time to think things through. Remember, you are not perfect. No one is. You're human. Every human being makes mistakes or needs to improve in some way.

3. Think: how can I use this?

Before you accept a criticism or dismiss it, ask yourself, 'How is this helpful?' Think: what is the useful information here? A negative comment on what you're wearing at work might mean you do need to smarten up your act. But when someone makes the same comment on your Instagram, you can likely ignore it. If a comment does contain helpful information, ask yourself: how can I use this to up my game? It might even be worth asking the other person for more specifics of what and how you could do better.

4. Say 'thank you'

Remember it may have been a challenge and an act of courage for the other person to offer their feedback. So 'thank you' is almost always the best response. Feedback can be a gift. Be grateful for criticism if its intention is to help you. Think of it as a brilliant resource to help you to get better. If you want to become great at something, you won't get there without feedback.

Even if the criticism comes from some illogical person trolling you online and you intend to ignore the 'feedback', thanking them is still the best way to go (nothing will irritate them more).

5. Admit to and acknowledge your faults

This can also be part of doing the work to own your shadow, like we did in Chapter 22 'Owning your shit'. When you do this, negative feedback won't surprise you, because you'll already have explored and accepted those parts of yourself.

6. Be kind to yourself

Yes, it may hurt. But the feedback (if it's constructive) is about what you did, not who you are as a person. You are multifaceted and complex, and you cannot be judged or defined by someone else. Be gentle with yourself.

· ·

Exercise: write a praise list

It's easy to walk out of a meeting feeling crestfallen at negative feedback, even if it was only 5 per cent of the total feedback, and the rest was encouraging. Because of 'negativity bias', our natural tendency as humans is to remember the criticism and discard the praise (it's all about survival, remember). So make a conscious effort to note down and reinforce any positive feedback. Create a 'praise list' of your good points and review it often to reinforce the fact that any criticism doesn't define you. Write down all the compliments you've received, good feedback, successes, things you're proud of and challenges you have overcome, and add to it every week, reviewing it each time.

· ·

Summary

★ If you get interrupted, saying 'one moment' or just continuing to speak can help you to finish what you were saying.

★ Going down, instead of up, at the end of a sentence can help you to sound more credible.

★ Saying 'thank you' to criticism is always the way to go. Ask yourself how you can use criticism to help you.

CHAPTER 30

How to ask for what you want

Ask for what you want and be
prepared to get it!
MAYA ANGELOU

Asking for anything can be scary. It can make us feel vulnerable. Perhaps you feel as though you 'should' be perfect and therefore don't need help. Perhaps the thought of a refusal seems too much like a painful rejection. Or you're scared of what the other person will think of you.

By asking, we're putting ourselves out there. I speak to lots of women who hate to appear vulnerable. They can't bear the thought others might think they're weak or don't have their shit together.

The truth is that being vulnerable and being able to lay out your needs, wants, fears and weaknesses and ask for what you need, makes you one badass mother. Being vulnerable takes strength. And asking takes courage but can pay off big time.

The asking strategy that works is, to let yourself feel all the feelings, then take action anyway. It's about getting used to the idea that just because you feel uncomfortable, it's not time to retreat or run away, contrary to what the adrenaline pumping through your body is telling you.

From bitch to badass

Although it's changing, we still live in a world where confident girls are labelled 'bossy' and assertively asking for what you want can mean you're called a bitch. While it won't happen overnight, we can all do our bit to speed up the change in our collective consciousness when it comes to confident women. It starts with supporting each other and championing each other's success. It means not interrupting each other and learning to be inspired by strong women rather than needing to tear them down. We need to stop calling other women bitches because the word is dehumanizing. It means a female dog, after all. Is someone a 'bitch' because she got what you wanted? Because she has a different opinion than you? Because she had the confidence to ask and you didn't? No. Let's just delete this word from our lexicon. I prefer the term badass. Badass women feel the fear but ask anyway. They know their worth and what they want, and they're prepared to get it.

You deserve what you're asking for

Self-doubt is a big reason we're reluctant to ask for things. 'I often find it hard to ask for what I want, and that's usually because my self-doubt kicks in to tell me I'm not deserving of it,' says Suzanna, a marketing executive, aged twenty-seven. 'I mostly struggle to ask friends for emotional support as I feel they probably don't want to hear about my issues when they're dealing with their own.'

If you've been a people pleaser or had imposter syndrome, asking for what you want can feel nails-on-a-blackboard awful. But as a human being, you deserve to have your needs met.

You deserve to be paid well for your hard work and experience. You deserve to be listened to and given help as much as the next person.

Chances are, you're happy to listen to others, so what makes you so special that only you don't deserve that? Remember all the times that you've listened to and helped others, when you've dropped everything to go over to your heartbroken friend's flat with prosecco and snacks. When you've listened intently to a friend in need. Or gone to a hospital appointment with them. Held their hair back while they vomited into the loo. Or helped them to move house. Chances are, you've done a lot for other people and you might find they're delighted to offer some support in return. Most likely, people would hate the idea of you suffering alone or in silence because you were afraid to ask for help.

Asking for help from a professional is also tricky for a lot of us. Far from being selfish or self-indulgent, getting professional help if you're struggling with your mental health or your relationship could be one of the best investments you make. You might ask yourself: 'Who am I to spend this money on something so self-indulgent?' But I believe that we all need help at some stage or other in our lives. If your car kept stalling, you wouldn't hesitate to spend the money to get it fixed, would you? You might be reluctant, but you'd spend the cash rather than drive around in a car that's about to break down. The same goes for your mind. Arguably, there's nothing more important than our mental health, so it makes sense to get help from someone who is trained to guide you out of the pattern of mental anguish.

I would also argue, if you are struggling to keep the house clean or do your life admin or you need childcare, get help. It's OK to ask friends and family for this. If you're in a position to be able to afford it, it's more than OK to pay someone to support you, whether it's a cleaner or PA. If finances don't permit, can you do a skill swap with a friend or come to an arrangement where you help each other out?

Summary

★ Asking for what you want can be scary – but we can feel the fear and ask anyway.
★ Asking for help is not selfish or indulgent – taking care of yourself is essential.

CHAPTER 31

Asking for what you want at work

This chapter is mainly about work because that's where our work and skills are swapped directly for money, so it's the most obvious place your value is measured. Knowing your strengths and the value you provide will give you the self-belief to go after what you want at work. But it's also key in life too: in relationships, friendships and for your own self-esteem.

We all have unique abilities and talents, areas where we excel. They could be as big as having an incredible mind for business or as small as being able to remember people's names. Sometimes we dismiss what we're good at, don't recognize its value because it feels too easy and we've been taught value only comes from hard work. We don't grasp that while a skill might feel like second nature for us, it could be challenging for other people. Maybe you have a great ability to put others at ease, organize your diary, prioritize or keep your clients loyal. Perhaps you're skilled at spreadsheets, or cooking is effortless to you. Maybe you're a brilliant listener, incredibly organized or an amazing timekeeper. Not everyone is able to do these, so if you can, give yourself credit.

· ·

Exercise: uncover your strengths

Once you've followed the steps below, you'll have a full list of your strengths. Review them every week, and particularly before you go into a situation when you have to ask for what you want.

What do you believe your strengths are?

What would your best friend say your strengths are?

What would your mum or dad say?

What would your manager or your team say?

What would your dog say?

What is easy for you that others find difficult?

What else are you good at?

What else?

. . . .

Are you being paid what you're worth?

Even with all your strengths, skills, training and experience, you may not be being paid fairly. The pay gap is real. Government data in the UK (compiled by the Government Equalities Office) found that nearly eight out of ten women in 2018 work for a company that pays them less than their male counterparts.[1] This is a complex issue that I'm not going to attempt to solve here. There are myriad underlying reasons, including a lack of flexible working opportunities, women being more likely to work part time and do more unpaid labour such as childcare and housework, and the fact that traditional 'female' or 'caring' roles tend to be less well paid than traditional male roles.

In the past it was thought that the pay gap was in part due

to women being less likely to ask for more money. But a 2018 report by the *Harvard Business Review* found that women do ask for pay raises as much as men, but while women received one 15 per cent of the time, for men it was 20 per cent.[2] There is some hopeful news: for younger women, this gap seemed to disappear. But while this may be a sign of progress, there is still a way to go.

Is flexible working the answer?

Timewise and Deloitte published a 'manifesto for change' in 2018 that laid out how the key to eliminating the pay gap could be in increasing, destigmatizing and normalizing flexible working.[3] They found that allowing greater flexibility at work helped companies attract and keep the best people. This is good for the economy because it keeps people who need to work flexibly, including parents, in work and it's good for businesses as it saves money on desk space. Numerous studies suggest that flexible working and working from home boost productivity, happiness and motivation. One study of UK businesses by HSBC found that nine out of ten believed that flexible working was a bigger motivating factor for productivity than more money.[4] Happiness itself even boosts productivity. All of this adds up to important reasons why flexible working makes sense for employers.

When you need to work different hours because you're raising kids, looking after relatives or for your own mental health, flexible working is vital. But, sadly, it's not yet the norm. Deloitte's research has found the biggest barriers were outdated workplace cultures and stigma. Nearly a quarter of respondents to the survey said they felt their workplace culture was not supportive of flexible working, and 17 per cent believed working flexibly would stop them from progressing.

In fact, all employees have a legal right to ask for flexible working, not just parents or carers.[5] But my client Carla told me, 'Twice, I asked my manager if I could adjust my working day to attend therapy and he said no. I took it to HR and it was finally allowed but I still don't think my manager is happy about it.'

Presenteeism, the outdated, frankly ridiculous way of working where being seen at your desk is the measure of your work, rather than the actual quality of your work and your output, is still the norm. (Let's face it, a lot of those people are probably on Facebook!) But in addition, the newer culture of being expected to be available 24/7 for calls and late-night emails needs to change too. Be careful you don't cut your hours at work but end up being expected to do the same amount of work in less time.

Together, stress, depression and anxiety now make up the number one reason that people take time off sick from work. This way of working is crippling our mental health. Companies lose talented staff, who leave to preserve their work–health balance. And let's not forget how expensive it is for a company to have someone go off sick for stress, not to mention if they sue the company for causing that stress. If you are being expected to work beyond reasonable expectations, reread Chapter 12 'The strength of setting boundaries' for how to establish boundaries.

According to Timeless, nine out of ten employers are open to hiring a flexible worker.[6] Even when a job was advertised as full time, most managers said they were 'pleased' to get requests about working flexibly.

One issue is, many of us are too scared to ask. 'I do find it hard, especially if it's from a person with authority, and especially from my boss,' says Layla, twenty-eight, who works in sales. 'A while back, after much hand-wringing and a therapy session, I asked my manager if I could cut my hours. Beforehand, my fear of the interaction going badly had spiralled into anxious thoughts and almost prevented me from asking at all. It turned out he was perfectly nice and reasonable. Even though I didn't get exactly what I wanted, it taught me that pushing through the fear is better than suffering in silence, or feeling resentful because I hadn't made my wishes clear. So now I am up for asking, whatever it is for.'

If we don't ask, we definitely won't get. But when we're brave enough to ask, we might just get what we want. And, in the process, we can change the culture not only for our own benefit but for that of others, too.

Here are some ways to support flexible working:

- Stand up to dinosaur managers about the culture of presenteeism. Call out those who actively block flexible working.
- If you're a leader, be a role model for flexible working so that others feel more able to ask for it.
- Don't assume your managers will refuse your request or that flexible working wouldn't work for you. How could it work for you?
- Challenge expectations about old ways of working. Life has changed so much in recent years, why should the old rules about being at your desk 9 a.m. to 6 p.m. still apply?
- Encourage men to ask for flexible working too so it becomes the new normal.

How to ask for a raise

Have you ever avoided asking for more money? Was it for any of these reasons?

- Fear it will put your relationship with your manager at risk.
- Not wanting to come across as money hungry.
- Feeling uncomfortable about the negotiation process.
- Being afraid of losing your job.

Or perhaps simply not knowing you can ask is the main barrier.

Any or all of these reasons can come into play when we're asking for a raise or negotiating our pay at a new job. The scary thing is, if you fail to negotiate at every opportunity, such as when you get a job offer, take on more work, change job titles, are promoted or have an annual review, you could end up getting paid significantly less during the whole of the rest of your career.

I spoke to career experts Phanella Fine and Alice Olins from the Step Up Club, authors of *Step Up: Confidence, Success and Your Stellar Career in 10 Minutes a Day*. One issue they identify is that as a woman, 'you are coming from a position of weakness. Because bosses know that women don't like asking for money and so they will offer less money than to a man just because they don't expect you to negotiate. In effect, you are in a position where you like to negotiate less but you need to do it more! Remember, you are not alone – most of us don't like it. Even people who have confidence in other areas find this tough.'

Six steps to asking for a raise

1. Know your worth

Spend some time researching what others are earning. Are you being underpaid for your role? Check job sites to find out what the going rate is for similar positions and experience levels. Phanella and Alice say, 'Call some recruiters and have a conversation to find out what a reasonable amount of money would be. And speak to people you know in the industry [but not in your company] about what they earn.' Write down the relevant facts and figures on a piece of paper so you can refer to it while you negotiate.

2. Know why you're asking

Phanella and Alice advise, 'It's useful to have a reason beyond wanting to be paid more. It makes it easier to strengthen your resolve. So think: what will the money do for me? It could be for your kids, buying a house, or a business you want to fund. If you find yourself wanting to give up and thinking, 'Fine, I don't need the money,' go back to your reason.

3. Prepare your case

Ask yourself the following questions and write down your answers so that you can return to them.

- What is it you have to offer?
- What are your strengths?
- What have you achieved?
- What extra value could you add to the company?
- Have you taken on extra responsibility?

- Are you managing more people or covering a bigger area of the business?

4. The language you use is important

Starting sentences with 'sorry', or including qualifiers such as 'just' and 'actually' can make you appear uncertain and could, therefore, undermine your confidence.

5. Timing is everything

This might seem obvious, but having an awareness of what's happening in the company is key. Choose your moment; if the business just lost a key client, or they're making redundancies, it's probably not the best time to ask for more cash.

6. Decide on your next move

Consider what you will do if you don't get the raise you feel you deserve. Ask yourself:

- Is there a lower amount that you are willing to accept?
- Are you prepared to walk away if you don't get what you want?
- Do you have other offers on the table?

Getting paid vs working for free when you're self-employed

If you're self-employed or work in the creative industries, there is a disappointing trend of being expected to work for free. But getting exposure in return for your hard work isn't going to put avocado toast on the table or get you closer to your goal of owning your own home. I've been asked to work for free by huge, massively profitable companies. While in some cases I've judged it to be worthwhile if they're able to promote my work widely through the company, in other cases I have decided my time would better be spent elsewhere.

It's important for you to draw your own boundaries: what would make working for free worthwhile for you? Might it be, for example, if an incredible company could give you a testimonial or you could sell a high-value product at a speaking gig you're giving for free? Maybe it would be for a cause you believe in or you would genuinely gain valuable experience? But if it's hard to see what's in it for you, or you think you'll end up resenting it, it's OK to say no thanks or ask to be paid. If you're unsure, consider the following:

- Remember all the investment you've made in your training and experience; all the time, money, blood, sweat, late nights and tears it's taken for you to get to where you are today. It wasn't 'cheap' for you to get to where you are; why should you sell your services for free?
- When we agree to working for free in the future, next month or next year, it can seem like an abstract idea. Instead, imagine that it's about to happen on Tuesday. Do you resent having to do it now? Would you rather have that free time than the free exposure? This mind switch will help you to figure out if you'll regret saying yes.
- Do your research and find out what others are getting paid for similar gigs so you're not selling yourself short. Often freelancers are happy to

share this sort of information; we are all in this together!

- A friend of mine says she feels awkward talking about money. So she's created a PDF of her services, detailing exactly what she can offer and how much she charges. When someone enquires about her work, she sends over her rate sheet.
- If you feel uncomfortable talking money, plan what you will say beforehand. Your stock question could be: 'Do you have any budget for that?' If the answer is no, this statement can work fine: 'I don't have the capacity to do any unpaid work at the moment, but thank you anyway.'

Summary

★ Remembering your strengths and the value you provide will empower you to feel more confident.

★ Almost nobody enjoys asking for money or better hours; remembering why you're asking can help.

CHAPTER 32

Making conflict work for you

In your head, you've imagined the difficult conversation in gut-churning detail and played out all possible reactions the confrontation could lead to. Your hands feel clammy at the mere thought of the possible escalation, maybe to tears and/or an angry outburst. But if you're doing everything in your power to avoid the discomfort of a disagreement, you could be missing out on finding a resolution as well as ignoring your needs. What's more, if there's an injustice, when we keep quiet about it, it's almost as though we are condoning it.

It can take real courage to face your fear of confrontation head on. Whether it's a political conversation, big work meeting, discussing the distribution of domestic chores with your house-mate or telling your boss you're overworked and can't take on any more, they are all potentially inflammatory. Not to mention those situations where a friend is being casually racist, or a colleague makes a sexist remark. Whether at work or at home, it's not surprising we fear these sorts of conversations.

I used to find criticism so painful, I would avoid confrontation at any cost. I'd shut down conversations by reacting with hurt or anger. Friends and family learned not to raise issues with me because it never ended well. What I've since realized is this: I don't want to be someone who people feel afraid to have difficult discussions with. Because without having those conversations, we stay stuck and oblivious to our wrongdoings. Really, we are hurting the people that we care about, as they won't feel able to express themselves and get their needs met.

Instead, I want to be the sort of person who people feel they can talk to openly, even when the conversation feels confrontational. These days, I go out of my way to welcome feedback and ask for it from clients and after the workshops that I deliver. My partner Aidan and I have regular discussions about our relationship, checking in with each other and asking for feedback. I consciously remember I don't need to be perfect, and I aim to always be open to learning and changing. I don't know about you, but I'd much rather things were said to my face than behind my back. At least then, I'm armed with the knowledge to change.

Gemma, thirty, an account manager, told me about a work conflict. 'Like almost everyone, I don't like confrontation. I recently had to stand my ground with a new boss who was dismissive of a new process I wanted to establish. I could see how it would make the business more efficient and ultimately lucrative. But he met my idea with condescension and disrespectful language. I was so passionate about the change, I continued to push my opinion. Eventually the boss conceded. I was proven right: the change has had a positive effect on the whole team. This has only made me more determined to face conflict when it's necessary.'

It's kind to be clear

We might think we're saving someone else's feelings by not having a difficult conversation, but the opposite is true. Brené Brown in her book *Dare to Lead* says, 'Clear is kind, unclear is unkind.' Leaving someone in limbo because you haven't fully expressed your view can leave them confused and in the dark about what they did wrong. Cutting out a friend because it feels easier than telling them how they hurt you is not kind.

Neither is letting resentment fester inside, unexpressed, then unleashing the rage of your suppressed feelings. That is being unkind to yourself, too.

This is the perfect example of the lengths we'll go to, to avoid having an awkward conversation – and how self-destructive it can be. My client Stephanie, twenty-seven, told me, 'I've recently bought a flat. What I didn't know before I moved in, is that the walls are thin and one neighbour's surround sound is so loud it vibrates my whole living room! I want to tell him, but I don't know how or what to say. I tend to overthink and I have built myself up into such a state that I'm scared I'll end up blurting out the wrong thing. At this point, my mind is even telling me to sell the flat rather than confront him!'

Getting set up for difficult conversations

I recently watched an interview by feminist journalist Helen Lewis, debating with clinical psychologist Jordan Peterson, who has some very different views to her. I was struck by how calmly and elegantly she was able to argue her point of view and I was intrigued to know how she prepared for such challenging conversations.

She told me, 'It's about acknowledging something is going to be difficult before you start – but deciding it's important enough that you are going to do it anyway. It's useful to have a measurement within yourself about what is important to you and what is important for you to do or say. Then before you embark on the difficulty, you think about that.'

So, remembering your values and the 'why' of the conversation is vital. Are you having the conversation to uphold your value of fairness, truthfulness, kindness or respect? Is raising an issue with a friend, at root, about how much you appreciate your friendship? Is asking for more money really about you valuing your time and energy? Tune in to that before you head into the potential confrontation.

Helen adds that tapping into our values helps us to care less about what others think. 'Other people's opinions matter much less when you've got your own star you're aiming for in mind and an idea of your goals and reasons for doing that.'

Knowing and accepting yourself, faults and all, which is something we explored in Chapter 22 'Owning your shit', is another tool in being able to handle these challenges. Helen says, 'If you are expecting the criticism, it doesn't hurt as much because you've factored it in already. You know people aren't going to like what you say, so it doesn't take you by surprise.'

Reframe confrontation

What if a little conflict could be, in fact, an opportunity? A chance for things to get better? What if you standing up to someone will have a positive effect on other people? A conflict could even end up being a bonding experience that improves your relationship with the other person – kind of like when you and a new partner have your 'first fight' but grow closer as a result!? Being able to stand up for yourself, assertively ask for what you want or challenge someone might just earn you their respect. And for you, bravely facing up to the difficulty of conflict will empower you to know what you're capable of.

I spoke to executive coach Charlotte Dewhurst, a self-confessed lover of difficult conversations (or at least of their benefits). Her technique is to put things in perspective beforehand. Ask yourself: 'What's the worst that could happen? Will this person's reaction matter in a year from now?' Another way she suggests you prep is to practise with a friend. She wants us to get used to conflict by setting targets for it each week, which spell out which conversations you'll have. 'Which conversations will you prioritize and which will you let go? How many difficult conversations will you have each week? This isn't about becoming too confrontational, but about flexing your muscles and practising, as well as defending your values when they really matter.'

Steps for handling confrontation

Here are some strategies for handling confrontation that will help you be prepared and boost your chances of achieving a successful outcome.

- Give them the benefit of the doubt. Rather than blaming or criticizing the other person, assume they are doing their best. They may be unaware of how the issue is affecting you, or they may themselves have a good reason for what they're doing. Instead of making a judgement, get curious about what's going on and try to see it from their perspective.
- Plan what you'll say beforehand so you make the points you want. Consider practising with a friend too.
- Use non-violent communication, which I'll describe in Chapter 34 'How to communicate your needs'.
- Keep breathing. It may well be nerve-wracking, but making sure you keep taking deep, belly breaths will calm your nervous system.

- Start small. Is there a small 'risky conversation' you can have, such as setting a boundary, saying no or making a request, that will build your confidence for bigger, harder conversations?
- Write it down. If confronting someone face to face seems like an impossible task, and you're certain your emotions would take over, a carefully worded letter or card could allow you to express yourself with calmness and clarity.

• •

Exercise: confronting yourself

This exercise allows you to open up about how conflict avoidance has left you stuck. Think of an issue, then answer the following questions:

Where have I been avoiding confrontation?

What could the possible benefits be of raising this issue, or having this difficult conversation?

What are the main points I'd like to make during this conversation? Can I script some of it out beforehand? Practise with a friend?

What is the worst thing that could happen in this conversation? What would be the best outcome?

• •

How to respond to rude people

We've all experienced rudeness, only to find that hours later, we come up with the perfect comeback! But instead of kicking yourself for not thinking of that clever or perfect answer at the time, you can prepare yourself in advance by deciding what you want to say to rude or unkind people.

Like most women over the age of twenty-five, I'm constantly getting asked when I'm getting married or having children. Recently, a friend of the family even said 'tick tock' to me! Comments like this can catch you off guard and leave you reeling – or mean you blurt out something you later regret.

Be cautious; don't lose your head in your need to be right. Remember the saying, 'everyone is fighting a hard battle'. Try not to take rudeness personally as it might be unintentional, or the person lashing out at you is doing so for their own reasons, their bad day, bad week or even bad life. They may be judging you through their own misconceptions or just acting out their own pain or stress. Sometimes rudeness is actually social awkwardness in disguise. Or they might be having an oblivious moment, as we all do at times. Sometimes, the best and kindest response might be to ignore them or walk away. It might even be you who's being the rude one! If someone angrily calls you a bitch as you accidentally knock their bag on the bus, it might be wise to keep quiet and not inflame the situation. Other times, you have to be brave enough to call it out. When that's the case, there are some handy strategies you can employ.

Say it like it is

Don't be afraid to say, 'I think you are being rude/unprofessional/unkind.' For example, when someone makes an unwanted comment about your appearance/weight/outfit, reply, 'Ouch – that's not very kind!'

Point out the ridiculousness
of what they just said

For example, if someone's made a backhanded comment about your weight by asking, 'Do you really think you should eat that?' you can reply (in an incredulous tone), 'Did you actually just ask me if I should eat this?' Or, 'I can't believe you just asked me that!'

Tell them it's none of their business

If someone asks, 'When are you going to have children?' you can reply, 'That's a very personal question!' This goes for the question, 'Why are you still single?' A lot of people I spoke to told me this can be a pretty hurtful – not to mention irritating – question. The implication is, there has to be something wrong with you, not that you haven't yet met the right person or are choosing to ride solo. 'Because I choose to be,' or, 'I'm fussy!' are both great responses.

Turn it back on them

This is a way to respond to the single question too: 'I don't know, why don't you tell me?' Hopefully this will highlight the inappropriateness of their question; although it could backfire and prompt more rudeness. Someone also suggested this gem: 'I enjoy being single and I'm not bothered by social constructs, but it's interesting that you are. Why do you think that is?'

. . . .

Exercise: **prepare your rudeness replies**

Think of some situations where you might face, or have dealt with, a rude comment. Plan a brave response to each.

Summary

★ Avoiding conflict means issues don't get resolved, and this could be doing you both a disservice.
★ It's kinder to be clear about your boundaries and what you want.
★ Confrontation can be an opportunity for things to get better.

CHAPTER 33

How to stand up for what's right

If you're fortunate enough not to be affected by racism or discrimination of any kind, it's all too easy to assume this is not your battle to fight. But this is a luxury that many people don't have.

If we're in such a privileged position, it is still absolutely our responsibility to defend others who are discriminated against. The people affected don't have the privilege of turning their heads away and ignoring it. I'm not suggesting you need to be a hero and try to break up a fight or put your own safety at risk, but I do think you should let people know when what they're doing or saying isn't OK.

A client of mine, Sarah, thirty-two, who works for a media agency, told me about a colleague who'd make sexist comments to her and other women in her male-dominated office. 'He asked me to wear a short skirt to a client meeting and told me "not to have a hissy fit" when I raised an issue. So the next time he crossed a line, I asked him, "Would you say that to a man?" He looked pretty sheepish.' Obviously, standing up for things can feel risky, but the more we collectively do it, the easier it will get – and the less likely it will be to happen in the first place.

Discrimination is often less about out-and-out aggression and more about subtle, everyday comments and questions. These have a name: micro-aggressions. Most people aren't even conscious they're doing them. But even these small things can add up, and damage a person's self-esteem.

The person doing the micro-aggression might have good intentions or just be oblivious to the hurt they're causing. All of us have unconscious biases that can mean we're offensive in ways that we're not even aware of. By pointing them out, you're doing the right thing, because even casual comments can be hurtful and feed into a culture where discrimination is acceptable. And only once we're aware of our biases, can we change them.

Examples might be:

- A woman being told she's 'hysterical' or to 'calm down, dear'.
- A person of colour being asked, 'Where are you *really* from?'
- Being told your name is 'too difficult' to pronounce.
- Being told, 'You don't look gay.'
- Someone asking intrusive questions about sex or their body to a trans person.
- Saying to a person of colour born in the UK, 'Your English is really good.'

It can take courage to accept responsibility for having offended someone. It's easy to be defensive when we're criticized, particularly if we weren't aware we were being offensive or discriminatory. But if someone accuses you, please do take it seriously. Listen with openness, think before you respond, and then go away and educate yourself with books, blogs or podcasts about the topic.

Have the courage to speak up

You can start by making the decision to be the sort of person who speaks up about these things. It's about connecting to your values and using that to inspire your courage. You might find it helpful to prepare what to say in certain situations, to give you more confidence.

- 'Why don't you leave him/her alone?'
- 'That sounds racist.' (You might also want to explain to the person why it sounds racist: perhaps because of our history, or because it supports a negative stereotype.)
- 'That makes me uncomfortable.'
- 'Would you call a man "sweetheart"?'

As I'll discuss in the next chapter, when I explain non-violent communication, it's important not to shame the other person or call them names, as this is likely to bring up their defences, and you won't get through to them. But more on this later.

Summary

★ It's our responsibility to stand up for other people.
★ Be aware of discrimination and micro-aggressions and don't be afraid to speak up about them.

CHAPTER 34

How to communicate your needs

My partner is not a fan of cleaning. That might be an understatement. He claims he doesn't 'see' the mess (hands up who knows someone like this – and hands up who has wanted to throttle them!). I used to keep my mouth shut, silently resenting him as he left a trail of destruction in his wake. Then, one hormonal day, I would always snap, loudly and angrily proclaiming that he never did any tidying and telling him how useless he was.

As you can imagine, this didn't go down well. As anyone who's ever been shouted at will know, when you're verbally attacked, you go on the defence. It's human nature. When we're blamed and criticized, we don't absorb what the other person is saying. When I blame Aidan for not tidying up, he gets defensive. 'You never take the bins out! And who do you think washes your underwear, the underwear fairy?!' I shout, exasperated. He replies, 'I was in a rush to get to work, you've been at home all day!' to which I yell, 'I've been at home working, I shouldn't have to clean up after you!' Cue an awkward dinnertime where both of us are in a grump, and the trail of destruction remains where it is.

When we're shouted at or aggressively criticized, we shut down, and look for ways to defend ourselves, from stonewalling to launching a counter-attack, blaming the other person or yelling a barrage of abuse. The result is, you lose your connection with the other person, the message doesn't get through, the bins don't get taken out, and no one is happy.

Non-violent communication

The great news is, there is a technique to getting your needs met that creates connection rather than alienation. Psychologist and visionary Marshall Rosenberg has nailed the art of asking for what you want, while still keeping the peace. In his book *Non-Violent Communication* he sets out the framework he created that allows people to express their needs and make requests without judging or blaming the other person. If you follow the rules of non-violent communication (NVC), he says, you'll find it easier to ask for what you want, and you've got a better chance of getting it. It works for any-size issue, from asking your housemate to stop drinking your milk, to raising the issue of sexism in your office.

Step 1: convert judgements to observations

The first step of NVC is to make an observation about the other person, rather than a judgement. When you judge, you damage the sense of connection between you. My old story used to be: 'Aidan has selfishly left his clothes all over the floor because I don't matter to him.' This is clearly a judgement, not an observation of the facts. An observation would be: 'I see Aidan has left his clothes on the floor.' This is less emotionally charged and therefore less likely to trigger defensiveness in the other person.

Here are some examples of judgements vs observations.

- You never listen to me! → I see you looking at your phone when I try to talk to you.
- You're selfish and uncommitted! → I notice when

245

I bring up the topic of moving in together, you change the subject.

- My family don't matter to you. → We visited your parents four times this year and mine only once.
- You don't appreciate anything I do for you. → I see you often get up from the table without thanking me for cooking.
- You're a racist arsehole! → I noticed you made a comment about immigrants earlier.
- You're a bad friend. → You didn't get back to me after I called you five times.

Step 2: say how you feel

The next step is to voice how you feel. This is always related to what you feel in your own body, and not about what others might think or feel. Remember, no one can make you feel anything.

My old way of expressing this would be: 'Your messiness makes me so angry. And it shows you don't love me!' This is a judgement and also includes blame – which is understandably going to put Aidan into defence mode, so he's unlikely to do what I want. Instead, I want to express how I feel without blaming and without the old story. So I say, 'When you leave your clothes on the floor, I feel frustrated and unloved.' This way of phrasing things is powerful not only for others but for ourselves. It helps us to remember that we are responsible for how we feel, not someone else.

Here are some examples of blaming vs expressing feelings:

- You never want to do anything on the weekends! → I often feel lonely at the weekend.
- You always take her side! → I'm feeling unsupported.

- How could you get so drunk last night?
  → I'm feeling disappointed.
- You're such a critical person. → I am
  feeling hurt.
- You should know better than to say that.
  → I was uncomfortable with what you said.
- I really needed you and you weren't there
  → I was feeling really alone.
- You made me feel scared and uncomfortable.
  → When you said that, I felt scared and
  uncomfortable.

Step 3: **state your needs**

Next, express what your needs and values are. The 'need' explains why you feel the way you do. This relates to basic human needs rather than just a preference. The old Chloe might have said something like, 'You need to be tidier!' But instead, I say, 'I have a need to have a clear space to work from in order to feel calm.'

Here are some examples of needs and values:

- I have a need for security.
- I have a need to get a good night's sleep.
- I value security.
- I have a need for company at the weekend.
- I have a need for things to be fair.
- I really value being listened to.
- I have a need to feel appreciated.
- I have a need to feel safe at work.
- I have a need to be respected as a human being.
- I have a need to be listened to.
- I value equality.

Step 4: **ask for what you want**

Lastly, you make a request. The best way to phrase this, according to NVC, is to ask specifically for what you want.

Start your request with: 'Would you be willing/like to . . . ?'

- Would you be willing to put your clothes in the dirty clothes basket?
- Would you be willing to turn the music down so that I can sleep?
- Would you be willing to listen to me for a few minutes without interrupting?
- Would you like to spend Saturday evening together?
- Would you be willing to stop making comments like that?

Phrasing a request as 'would' or 'would you like' to do something, rather than 'you must' or 'you should' gives the other person the freedom to say no. And when people don't feel forced or pressured, are given the option to say no, they feel more connection and are therefore more likely to say yes.

Putting it all together, it looks like this: 'When . . . I feel . . . because I am needing/I value . . . would you/will you . . . ?'

Here are a couple of examples of how to put NVC into practice.

- When I see you looking at your phone when I'm talking to you, I feel frustrated. I really value being listened to. Would you be willing to put your phone down when we're talking?
- When you made that comment about immigrants, I felt really uncomfortable. I need to uphold the

values of tolerance and equality in our office.
Would you be willing to not use that language in future?

By following these suggestions, you'll be able to speak up and ask for what you want with your friends, family or partner, while keeping the peace and connecting to what you really need. And, win-win, you'll be giving yourself the best chance of them saying yes.

Getting your needs met in the bedroom

Even in the current climate of women's empowerment and body positivity, one place women struggle to ask for what they want, is in bed.

I asked sexpert and author Tracey Cox for advice. She told me: 'Whether you sleep with men or women, communicating what you want can be tricky. There are so many reasons we keep quiet. Maybe you're not sure other women ask for what they want in bed. Well, they do – and those that don't, should. Many men certainly don't sit back and wait for an orgasm or good sex to happen. Because we're more likely to be people pleasers, we're less likely to ask. They ask for what they want, move a hand to where it feels better, position themselves so it hits the right spot. Or maybe you don't ask because you don't want your partner to think you're suggesting they're anything but a perfect lover. Or you worry they'll see you as less sexy, less feminine or less desirable. Or that you're the only woman who needs, for example, clitoral stimulation (we all do!). Or perhaps you aren't experienced enough to figure out what you need.'

You can boost your confidence to ask for what you want in bed by following these four steps recommended by Tracey.

1. Start with research

The website OMGyes.com will give you an eye-opening look at the techniques real women use to orgasm and on traceycox.com you'll find practical tips too.

2. Be reassured

Any good lover is far more likely to be grateful for (tactful, kind) feedback than offended. Talking openly and honestly is crucial to keeping sex fresh and interesting in the long term.

3. Say what you want, not what you don't

Talk about what you want more of, not less. Instead of, 'I hate it when you don't spend enough time on foreplay,' say, 'I love it when you spend lots of time on foreplay.'

If you want more of the same, say exactly what you loved about it ('Wasn't it amazing to make love outside?').

4. Suggest, don't criticize

Gently suggest new things or change, rather than criticize. So it's, 'I love it when you give me oral. Can you do it for longer?' rather than, 'You never give me oral sex for long enough.'

Good things to say and try

'I love touching you.'

'Do you like it when I do it here/hard/soft/like this/like that?'

'Which way do you like it best – like this or that?'

'I love your bottom. Do you want me to spank it?'

'Do you want me to put a finger inside you?'

'Can I kiss you here?'

Demonstrate what you'd like done to you (for example, using your tongue on the palm of your partner's hand or sucking one of their fingers).

What not to say or do

'I hate it when you do that.'

'God, that's so irritating.'

'John/Jane used to do this thing with their fingers – could you give it a try?'

'The hottest sex I ever had was with this Swedish backpacker on a beach. Why don't we ever have sex on a beach?'

Shout, 'And you're rubbish in bed!' in the middle of an argument.

Say, 'Why don't we ever do that?' in an accusatory voice.

Deliver a criticism without a compliment before it. Use the word 'should' instead of 'could you?' or 'would you?'.

Say, 'That's not normal. I can't do that!' (What is hell to one person may be heaven to another – with the exception of something truly vile, then feel free to tell them where to go!)

Be insensitive to their limitations (if he only lasts a minute during intercourse, asking him to last half an hour is pointless).

Make dirty talk sound like a demand or criticism.

How to work that ask

What small challenges can you set yourself in order to grow your confidence in asking? By practising asking, you might learn that you receive more help and 'yes' answers than you were expecting. Otherwise, you'll learn that you can absolutely handle a 'no'.

Examples could be:

- Asking your partner to give you a massage
- Asking a friend if they'll listen to a problem you have for a few minutes.
- Asking to finish work at 4 p.m. on Friday to go to an appointment.
- Asking a colleague to take on a project of yours.
- Asking for help from a shop assistant in choosing clothes.

. . . .

Exercise: how to get good at asking

What challenges would you like to set yourself when it comes to asking for what you want? Write them below and, if you can, schedule them into your diary so you'll be sure to follow through.

. . . .

. . . .

. . . .

. . . .

. . . .

. . . .

Summary

★ Making a demand or a criticism usually doesn't lead to you getting what you want.

★ Non-violent communication is about communicating in a way that makes sure everyone's needs get met.

CHAPTER 35

How to grow your social confidence

Just believe in yourself. Even if you don't, pretend that
you do and, at some point, you will.
VENUS WILLIAMS

I always used to agree to go to parties but, minutes before we were about to leave, I'd be overcome with an intense urge to crawl into bed and shut out the world. My wild imagination would play out a whole series of potential social embarrassments:

- I'd see me standing with no one to talk to, pretending to study an exciting section of wallpaper to make myself look busy.
- I'd see me actually talking to someone but shyly fumbling for words, getting hotter and redder by the second as my inner critic stage-whispered all the reasons I was a bit shit into my ear.
- I'd see me attempting to approach a friendly-looking group of people . . . then see them all giving me a suspicious sideways glance and slowly inching away, leaving me standing alone, again.
- I'd see me bursting into flames with awkwardness, and a pothole conveniently opening up and swallowing me.

In my anxious state, all of the above seemed like perfectly reasonable possibilities. Then, after my boyfriend had grumpily left to go to the party without me, I'd proceed to beat myself up about wimping out. Not ideal. But I found the awkwardness of having to face new people too much to bear.

If you find social situations challenging, you'll likely feel a strong pull to avoid them too. The problem is, the more you try to run away, the more likely fear is to chase after you and bite you in the ass. Social connection isn't a nice-to-have, it's a must-have. Human beings are social creatures, and we need relationships in order to feel healthy and whole. Our relationships give us a sense of belonging – and this, in turn, boosts our confidence. 'Love and belonging' is the third most basic need in Maslow's hierarchy of needs, a model which describes what humans need the most. Only food, water, warmth and safety are more important to us!

Sadly, we're not getting what we need: rates of loneliness are now higher in young women than any other group. Social connection is so important; it's even thought that loneliness may reduce your life span as much as smoking or obesity.

I'm not saying you have to go to every party you get invited to – you don't. I know it isn't always possible to push through and make yourself go. Sometimes facing your fears can seem like too much. But you do need social interactions and relationships. You need people. So while you might just want to hang back and wait for the party or meet-up to be over, don't do what most of us do – what I did – and that's to make the situation much worse in our heads.

There are a few reasons why people hate parties. It could be social anxiety that's making the thought of speaking to people about as attractive as a sick bucket. Social anxiety is a fear of being judged. It ranges from nervousness about meeting new people to finding it so scary, it feels damn near impossible to get out of there intact. Or it could be low self-esteem or your inner introvert taking charge. Maybe you are scared people won't like you, or they'll think you're stupid, or you believe you were born 'shy' and will always be that way.

Regardless of where your fear of socializing comes from, I promise you it can change. We are all capable of feeling good around people. Learning social confidence is simply creating a personal arsenal of tools that can take you from boardroom to party to casual encounter on the street. Whether you need a serious social confidence overhaul or just want to feel more yourself with other people, these mindset shifts and practical tools will empower you so you can talk to anyone. The keys are to enjoy being you when you're with others and to trust yourself to do your best during social interactions. And remember, your reward for taking action will be confidence.

Avoid avoiding and expect the best

Trust me, avoiding any social situation because of fear about how it'll go makes things way, way worse. When you do this, whether it's a party, after-work drinks or a coffee morning with your mum-friends, you send yourself a message: this is a dangerous situation I should steer clear of.

If you do actually go to the party or meet-up, have you ever noticed when you get there, it's usually . . . drum roll . . . fine? Often, I've found it's pretty great. These days, instead of imagining the worst, I've trained myself to expect the best or, at the very least, it'll be bearable. I picture myself confidently starting conversations, listening intently, smiling and laughing and having a good time. I remind myself of all the brilliant experiences I've had in social situations and how, most of the time, they've turned out fine. This makes me go into them feeling way more confident and positive than if I was expecting the worst.

Remember too, you will not be the only one in that social situation who has had to crowbar themselves out of their bed to be there. You're not the only one who's feeling wobbly. Parsha, thirty-four, says no one would ever guess she lacks confidence: 'I'm able to "play" the game very well. Nobody has any idea I'm so anxious about meeting people, both one on one and in a group. Behind closed doors, before every event, you'll find me regretting every "yes" to an invitation. But when I get there, I've found it's never as bad as I'd thought it would be. So remember, people will like you. And you might even enjoy yourself!'

• •

Exercise: the future you meditation

Try this simple meditation to help boost your social confidence.

Get comfortable, close your eyes and take some deep breaths. With each out breath, imagine your body relaxing a little more.

Imagine it's a few weeks or months into the future and you're feeling more socially confident than ever before. Feel your confident posture, standing tall and with open body language. Hear the positive thoughts you're telling yourself. Feel yourself breathing deeply and easily.

Imagine confidently introducing yourself to someone and asking them questions. Hear the clear and articulate sound of your voice, feel the words flowing easily. Notice yourself making eye contact, smiling and laughing.

Doing this sends a powerful message to your subconscious mind. It's a mental rehearsal that will train you to feel like this in real-life situations.

• •

Interested vs interesting

Curiosity is the antidote to anxiety. When we're lacking in confidence, it's as though we've already decided how the situation will go: badly. Instead, cultivate a mindset of curiosity. Imagine you're an explorer of life, heading out to see human beings in their natural habitat. Wonder about who you'll meet and what will happen. Set off on a voyage of discovery about the other person. Get curious about how you'll handle the interaction. Think of it as an adventure.

Instead of feeling you have to be interesting, work on being interested. In one study, published in the *Journal of Social and Clinical Psychology*, people who were curious and showed an interest in others came across as more appealing than those who didn't, regardless of their level of social anxiety.[1]

The best way to be instantly curious? Use open questions starting with: 'what', 'when', 'why', 'who', 'where' and 'how'. This will get the conversation flowing. But even more importantly, you need to really listen. I mean, REALLY listen. The format of most conversations is each person waiting for a turn to speak. As people don't often get a chance to be truly heard, your full attention is a tremendous gift to give. By listening, you'll build a much better relationship than if you're distractedly trying to formulate your interesting reply.

Remember your 'why'

I get a lot of courage from remembering that by speaking up, sharing my story and pushing through my discomfort and worry about what other people think, I can be an inspiration for someone else. The lesson behind this is, we get a lot of strength to do hard things when we remember *why* we're doing them.

So, what is the reason you want to get out there and speak to people? To make friends, get new clients, build your social confidence, expand your horizons, be a good partner or to have an exciting experience? Whatever it is, remembering *why* you want to go to the party or work event will help to motivate you and allow you to access your inner courage. Build up a vivid image in your mind of you achieving your 'why'. How will you feel once it's over and it went well? What will you enjoy the most? What opportunities could it lead to?

. . . .

Exercise: set yourself a small challenge

Remember, confidence is the prize you win when you chal-lenge yourself. What are some small steps you can take to start to grow it? Make a list of at least three challenges you can set yourself and schedule them into your diary. If this seems scary, remember how good you'll feel afterwards. Being specific about exactly what you'll do, or how long you'll stay, can help this feel more manageable.

Examples might be:

'I'll go to the networking event and stay for half an hour.'

'I'll introduce myself to three new people at the engagement party.'

'I will smile at, make eye contact with and acknowledge everyone in the meeting.'

'I will say hello to one of the other mums in the school playground.'

. . . .

Work on being a calmer you

I say this to all my clients. Working on being a calmer person generally will help you stay calm in social situations. If your nervous system is on high alert in your day-to-day life, going out of your comfort zone could push you into an anxious state. Make sure you're taking care of yourself while you work on your confidence. My first book, *The Anxiety Solution*, is full of strategies and insights into living a calmer life, so have a read if you haven't already. If your anxiety feels out of hand, speak to your GP and book in for some therapy.

For me, becoming calm was about making peace of mind my top priority. I've discovered regular meditation, nights in to recharge, and knowing when to say no are key for me. One thing I can't stress enough is the importance of being kind to yourself as you go through this process. If you struggle with something but you give it a try anyway, that's brave and worthy of respect. The end result isn't what matters, it's the willingness to try that deserves your love and compassion.

Calling all introverts

Have you ever considered you might be an introvert? It might explain why you find parties exhausting. And crowds. And even people! If you're not sure, see if the following description fits you. It's by Susan Cain, whose book *Quiet: The Power of Introverts in a World That Can't Stop Talking* set out to prove that introverts are just as happy and talented and successful as extroverts. She writes: 'Introverts may have strong social skills and enjoy parties and business meetings, but after a while wish they were home in their pyjamas. They prefer to devote their social energies to close friends, colleagues, and family. They listen more than they talk, think before they speak, and often feel as if they express themselves better in writing than in conversation. They tend to dislike conflict. Many have a horror of small talk, but enjoy deep discussions.'

Introversion is different from shyness. Shyness is where you may desperately want to be with other people, but fear prevents you from feeling comfortable to do so. While extroverts draw energy from being with people, introverts find social situations draining and recharge by being alone. As an introvert myself, I know I need time to rest and recharge.

According to Susan Cain, a third to a half of the population are introverts. And in our society, the qualities of extroverts are more highly valued than introverted ones. The loud people are the ones who get listened to, become leaders and often end up running the show. But the point is, just because you're a quieter person, it doesn't mean what you have to say has any less value. 'I try to remember that I am as important as the person/people to whom I'm speaking,' says Chrissy, twenty-nine, an introvert. Your strengths as an introvert may be in thinking, reflecting, being creative and having deep conversations as opposed to small talk. Remember that even though you might not be the loudest, your voice matters too.

Confidence strategies for introverts

It's totally possible to be a confident introvert, if you manage your energy levels and make sure you recharge alone after social time.

- Rather than attempting small talk, take advantage of your ability to think deeply in order to really listen and to ask meaningful questions that stimulate a deeper and longer conversation.

- Check in with yourself about how you're feeling and don't feel guilty about leaving once you've had enough or are starting to feel depleted.
- Schedule in time on your own before and after any big social occasions.
- If you've got a hugely social week at work, balance it with a very quiet and restorative weekend.

Summary

★ Fear shrinks when you walk towards it – so don't avoid the things you're afraid of.

★ In social situations, being curious and interested is much more important than trying to be interesting.

★ Visualize your future self feeling comfortable, confident and self-assured at a party, in a meeting, or on a date.

★ Working on being a calmer person generally will help you to stay calm and confident around people, so make self-care a priority.

CHAPTER 36

Put your adult in charge

As a kid, I thought that by the age of thirty-two I'd be adulting to the max, having life all figured out, with a house full of co-ordinated furniture and matching dinnerware. I thought I'd own my own home and have 2.5 children and a Ken doll lookalike husband. How wrong was I?! My plates and mugs are a mishmash, I've changed careers three times, and I'm still renting. There's still so much I have to learn about being a grown-up. The truth is, many people in their twenties and thirties still feel they haven't quite attained adulthood.

Can I speak to the adult in charge?

Have you ever walked into a room and felt like a child in an adult's body? Or, at a dinner party, as though you're a kid trying to talk at the grown-ups' table? Me too! A wedding or a workplace training day used to take me right back to being a shy eight-year-old, hiding behind my dad's corduroys.

Do a quick Google search and you'll discover you're not alone; 'I feel like a child' syndrome is a thing. People's social media feeds detail how they feel like 'a child in an adult's body' or discuss the strain of 'adulting' when they still, inside, feel like a teenager. Feeling inferior to other people, telling ourselves we're not good, experienced or smart enough to engage with other people, and having a strong desire to make a fort under the table to escape the mortgage chat, may be signs you might have the syndrome too.

The truth is, we all have a child inside of us. She'll always be there. Sometimes the childlike part of us is brilliant; helping us to play, be silly and laugh till our bellies ache. But sometimes we need to be the adult in charge.

I recently had to speak at an event when I wasn't feeling well, and I was extremely nervous. The child part of me was raging; I wanted to make a bed on Mum's sofa, sip warm Ribena and watch episodes of *Friends* while cuddling a hot-water bottle. But the adult part of me knew I had a job to do.

So I used a technique I call 'Adulting'. I adapted it from a type of therapy called Transactional Analysis, which works with the different parts of us we all have inside, namely an adult part and a child part.

First I imagined calling on the adult part of me to give my unhappy inner child part a big hug. Then I allowed the child part to step back, and the adult part to step forward. I thought through all the details of the adult part of me; the way she looks, dresses, speaks and acts. I imagined her saying, 'I've got this,' or, 'I'll take this from here!'

Finally, I began to act from the adult part of myself. I reminded myself of all the reasons I was, indeed, a competent and capable adult. Knowing that my adult self was now in charge gave me the strength to do the event. The next time you feel scared and overwhelmed, try calling on your inner adult part to comfort your inner child, too.

Make the first move

Recently I was invited to a wedding where I knew only the bride and groom. And, since Aidan was abroad for the week,

I had to go alone. As I've had my fair share of standing alone at parties, feeling hideously awkward and too shy to approach anyone, nose in my phone, desperately swigging prosecco, a wedding alone was basically my nightmare.

But this party, I decided, would be different. I was going to be an adult. And what would an adult do? Introduce herself to lots of people, of course. It helped that I already knew 40 per cent of people report themselves to be 'shy'. When you say hello to a stranger, there's a good chance they feel a bit nervous or awkward too – or can at least relate to that feeling.

I walked into the foyer of the town hall to find groups of people happily chatting and quaffing champagne. I had the old thought, 'Everyone already knows each other,' and the all-too-familiar urge to run away and hide in the loos. But I pushed it aside and (seemingly) confidently stuck my hand out to introduce myself to literally the nearest person, a man in his forties. I felt reassured when he looked relieved and the conversation flowed – in fact, he soon admitted he'd felt nervous and was glad I'd come to say hi!

These days, I make a point of being the one who approaches other people, assuming they might be a bit nervous too. So far, it's never failed. Making the first move puts you in control. It means no more waiting and hoping someone will speak to you. And as you take action, you prove to yourself you can be a confident person; you step into that role . . . and then you become it.

Fake it till you become it

No one wants to do the hard work of actually getting out there and just . . . doing . . . it. We love the idea that we can magically shift our mindset and be cured of any social nerves.

But the reality is, mindset will only take you so far. By far the best thing you can do to grow your social confidence is to get out there and be around people. Again, it comes down to retraining your nervous system. Once you teach it you can handle the discomfort, before long, meeting new people will feel like second nature.

Summary

★ If there are times when you still feel like a child or a teenager, imagine the adult part of you taking over and saying, 'I've got this!'

★ Make the first move and be the one to approach others first; it helps you feel more in control – and most people will be grateful when you do this.

★ Taking action is the fastest way to grow your confidence.

CHAPTER 37

How to talk to anyone

If you've ever found yourself wanting to bolt or your mind going blank when you're with a group of people, this section is for you. The reason for these symptoms is, you're in survival mode, fight or flight. In your brain, blood flow has moved away from the frontal cortex, the rational, clear-thinking part, and towards the muscles to help you run or fight. It's no wonder you can end up lost for words, blank or frozen.

How to prep for good conversations

Because it's harder to think clearly in those moments, there is no shame whatsoever in doing a bit of conversational pre-planning. Take a few moments to think about possible subjects or questions, for the times your rational mind inconveniently goes AWOL on you during a conversation. It could be a recent holiday you went on, your plans for Christmas or just asking, 'What have you been up to?'.

In her book *Captivate: The Science of Succeeding with People*, human behaviour investigator Vanessa Van Edwards shares examples of conversation starters which go deeper and flow better than the standard 'what do you do?' question so many of us dread. Keep these questions in the front of your mind before heading out to meet new people.

She suggests questions such as:

- 'How do you spend most of your time?'
- 'Have you been working on any exciting projects lately?'
- 'What are you excited about at the moment?'
- 'What plans do you have for the weekend?'
- 'What do you do to unwind?'

How to start a conversation with anyone

I was once terrified of any kind of networking including, as you already know, parties where there would be anyone I didn't know. If I went, I'd need to be thoroughly tipsy (read: drunk) before I'd attempt any kind of introduction. But my boyfriend, who used to work in sales and seems to have zero fear of stranger chat (those things may be linked) taught me a shockingly basic but highly effective formula for starting a conversation with anyone.

And it is . . . 'Hello, my name is Chloe.' It's not rocket science, but once I learned this was all I needed to start a conversation, it became loads easier. Once you've told them your name, they tell you theirs, and you can follow up with another question. Now, you're basically best friends.

Another sure-fire conversation starter is to give the other person a sincere compliment. If you like the look of someone and want to find an excuse to say hello, let them know you love their shoes or ask them where they got their balayage done. You can then introduce yourself . . . and the conversation will go from there. Obviously, make sure it's a real compliment; nothing fake here, please!

Summary

★ If you're worried your mind will go blank, prepare some questions in advance.

★ 'Hello, my name is . . .' are the four magic words to start any conversation.

How to find the real you and what she wants to do

CHAPTER 38

How to find your people

Who doesn't want to find their people? Those guys and girls whose weirdness matches your weirdness. Who make you double over with laughter in line at Costa, because their laugh is so freaking funny. Where one cup of tea (or glass of vino) turns into three. They cry at the same videos of baby animals sneezing as you. And you're able to share the things you've kept in your heart for ages – and be accepted for it. It's a beautiful feeling and one we all deserve to have. There is simply nothing else like being loved completely, just for being you. As human beings, we need this sense of belonging but, as I said before, we don't all have it.

Despite being hyper-connected in the digital world, so many people I speak to still feel lost, isolated and lonely. You might have plenty of small talk or chit-chat in the office, but lack the deep conversations you crave. It's time to put down your phone for a minute, to start being braver in your relationships.

One place I have personally found has changed my life, helped me go deep and form connections quickly is a sharing circle. This is exactly what it says: a group of people sit in a circle, share their struggles, challenges and what's showing up in their lives at that moment, usually with the help of a facilitator. It's part of the new movement for real connection, that's based on old practices – our ancient ancestors would have sat around a fire telling stories too. There are other, similar set-ups, such as support groups including Alcoholics Anonymous and group therapy.

My friend Gemma Brady is founder of the women's circle Sister Stories. Gemma told me:

> I felt a huge draw to start a women's circle, even though both speaking up in the circle and leading it were almost my worst nightmares. The idea of multiple eyes being on me has always filled me with dread and horror. Through my work as a documentary maker, managing teams, I've had to do it, but I'd be anxious for days beforehand.
>
> The circle is like a rehearsal space where we're speaking from the heart and listening without judgement, although there's no pressure to speak. We drop all the small talk, posturing and pretending we're someone we're not. When I started, I used to tremble with fear but, over time, it's helped me to break through the barrier of using my voice.
>
> When we take a brave step towards being more open about what's really going on, it's a fast track to forming deep relationships. When you speak openly and vulnerably, people relate to your story. The circle gives us a sense of belonging to something. And unexpectedly, speaking in the circle has helped me to articulate myself confidently in all areas of my life.

Even though it can feel scary to share, it gets less scary. Sharing is almost like a muscle, in that when you exercise it, it gets stronger, just as Gemma describes. I have seen, in sharing circles and from the workshops I've led, how we gain inspiration and confidence from having our story met with acceptance and from knowing that we're not alone. The most common feedback Gemma hears from women is, 'I didn't know how much I needed this until I came.' It takes courage to speak up, but when we do we create intimacy, community and a sense of belonging, as well as building our bravery.

Check out Gemma's circles and see if there is one near

you at www.sisterstories.co. Or search on sites like Meetup or Eventbrite for other sharing or women's circles. If you're looking for a community, there is one waiting for you to join them.

Summary

★ Time on social media is not the same as face-to-face time with real people. We need inter-person interaction to feel connected.

★ Sharing circles are a powerful way to experience community, intimacy and connection.

CHAPTER 39

Be the real you

> Ultimately, social anxiety is the fear that
> whatever we're trying to hide will be revealed to
> everyone like a gust of wind sweeps away a bad
> toupee. We think there is something wrong
> with us and therefore try to conceal it.
>
> **ELLEN HENDRIKSEN,** *HOW TO BE YOURSELF*

One piece of confidence advice I often hear is: just be yourself! But there's nothing more unnatural than *trying* to be yourself. And if we lack social confidence, we often lose track of our authentic self. We shape ourselves to fit the person we're speaking to, say and do what we think they'd like, approve of, be attracted to.

I spent years adjusting who I was, censoring what I said for fear of saying the wrong thing. I was convinced I needed to appear perfect if I was going to be liked. The more I hid the real me, the more pressure and tension I felt about being 'found out'. As I'd act like everything was fine when it wasn't, people found me hard to get to know. It was not only exhausting but, by putting on a front, I wasn't being authentic.

If you hide the real you, you won't attract your people. When we show a bit of our true selves, open up about vulnerabilities, we're more likely to be liked by the people who really matter. Being authentic means bravely showing up as yourself and owning your imperfections. As Brené Brown says, 'Courage starts with showing up and letting ourselves be seen.'

Everyone is struggling with something. When we admit we're having problems with our child's behaviour and we feel out of control, or we're worried about the abyss growing between us and our partner, or we don't feel good enough at work because we just received some critical feedback – chances are we'll find out the other person may have felt that way at one point too. Openly sharing our challenges helps put other people at ease – and we can relax more because we're able to be honest. EVERYONE is struggling with something. Pretending that everything is perfect when it isn't, is inauthentic. When we open up about the fact we're struggling and are inevitably met with a 'me too', we feel connected.

This isn't about oversharing; I'm not suggesting you tell a stranger the intimate ins and outs of your sex life in an attempt to build a connection with them, no! Burdening someone with your life story the first time you meet them is probably not the best idea (unless you're paying them and they're a trained therapist). You'll know when it's appropriate to share because it will feel comfortable and right. I'm saying that being your perfectly imperfect self and taking off your social armour may well foster more connection and so confidence. They'll see the real you and you'll realize you're accepted for who you are.

Making friends

As we grow up, most of us are thrown together with a ready-made group of potential mates – in our class, around our neighbourhood, in university halls or on our course.

But in adulthood, making new friends can seem tough. It might look as though everyone we meet is already sorted for friends. It's easy to drift away from old friends – people move, people change, have babies or shift their priorities – but it can feel much harder to meet new ones. Maybe most of your old friends enjoy going clubbing, but now you're looking for a quieter life. Or maybe they've settled down and moved to the country but you're still single and ready to mingle. As we get busier, it's harder to connect regularly. Making plans to meet up can seem like a battle of the diary schedules.

The result? You feel lonely. Research published in the UK in 2018 by the Office for National Statistics found that young people were the loneliest age group, with 10 per cent of 16- to 24-year-olds reporting that they were 'always or often' lonely.[1] The statistics showed renters tend to be lonelier than home-owners, and women lonelier than men. Having a mental health issue such as anxiety or depression can add to the feeling – it may lead to feeling isolated or misunderstood. Many of the people I've spoken to have even said worrying about the way they look stops them from going out and so contributes to feelings of solitude.

It's perfectly possible to be surrounded by people all day, at work, and still to feel alone inside if you're not getting the sense of belonging you crave. Social media is a great place to connect with people, but the flip side is, it can give a false connection that leaves us feeling a bit empty and lacking in nourishing face-to-face time, a biological need.

One of my favourite ways to make new friends as an adult has been to message people on social media and ask them to go for a coffee. This is quite normal in the world of the self-employed, since we're usually free during weekdays and can chat about the shared challenges and perks of working for yourself. But it's entirely possible to do at other times if you work for someone else too, or if you're a full-time mum.

Making friends does require you to put yourself out there and be a bit vulnerable. To ask the person you've been DM'ing on Instagram about your shared love of vintage fashion if she wants to meet in real life. To ask your girl crush from Body-pump if she wants to go to this other class you've found. Or to reach out to that friend of a friend you think you have loads in common with, to go on a girl date.

Ask yourself, what's the worst thing that can happen? They could say no, or that they're busy, or if it's on digital they might just ignore you. These are small prices to pay for the chance of years of incredible friendship with someone you totally dig.

My friend Amy Rushworth, a confidence coach, recently moved to the UK from Australia. Her strategy is to go to events where she thinks she'll meet like-minded women, then strike up a conversation. If she resonates with someone, she invites them for a coffee or to another event. And sometimes, she tells me, she even says, 'I know this is a bit weird, but would you like to be friends?'!

Remember the section about learning from role models in Chapter 27 'Why role models matter'? Who do you know that's amazing at making friends or at meeting new people? What do they do and how do they do it? How can you gain inspiration from them to be more socially confident?

There are loads of potential new friends out there, waiting and wishing that they could meet someone like you, to chat about your shared love of fitness or crystals, or *Bake Off*. Taking a little action in this area may just lead to surprising results.

Here are some places your potential new BFF could be hanging out:

- Yoga classes, retreats and workshops
- On social media, in Facebook groups and the Instagram comments of people you follow and mutually admire
- Entrepreneurship workshops and events

- Gym classes, running clubs and fitness communities like CrossFit
- Wellness workshops and events
- Meet-ups and Eventbrite events
- On the Bumble BFF app
- Mum groups
- Book clubs

. . . .

Exercise: begin your friend search

Brainstorm some ideas of where you could meet new people. Schedule one event into your diary. Decide beforehand to introduce yourself to some new people while you're there.

Summary

★ You create connections when you open up and allow the real you to be seen. Remember, everyone, like you, is struggling with something.
★ Loneliness is a big issue for young women – but you can make new friends.

CHAPTER 40

Stronger, wiser, smarter: how to be resilient

I just want to take a moment to remind you that you are, by nature, remarkably resilient. You are a human being: a woman, no less. You've survived an ice age, droughts, floods, you've built pyramids and rocketships. Potentially, you have the power to create life through your body, to grow tiny humans in your tummy and push them out of your vagina! You're a walking, talking, Instagramming miracle – and if you're not resilient, I don't know what is. It's just that you've forgotten. I want you to remember: you are a badass. A force of nature, one hell of a woman and . . . you've got this.

Resilience is your ability to bounce back from setbacks, big and small, to handle the challenging times but come back to a state of equilibrium. It's about how well you can adapt to the life changes we all go through. We need resilience to stand firm in the face of criticism, to keep going when we're doing something hard and when life doesn't work out as we'd want.

If you're a sensitive person, you might struggle with the idea of failure. Perhaps you're fearful of what people think of you, or you just don't feel very strong right now. That's OK. Resilience is something you can grow.

Remember I described the growth mindset back in Chapter 3 'Believe you can change'? This is where we learn to give things a try, rather than worrying about the actual result. Know this: getting back up after failure breeds resilience. What we may have once thought of as failure is actually a chance to learn and to become tougher. The same is true for feeling difficult emotions. It creates confidence that we can handle whatever comes up – aka resilience.

I have a confession: from a young age, I was a quitter. My parents wanted me to have a comfortable life and a better childhood than they'd had. They didn't want me to feel under any pressure, so when I hit a bump in life's road, they told me it was OK to give up. While this came from a lovely place, it meant within the space of five years, I quit piano lessons, guitar, Brownies, athletics, ice skating and creative writing.

What I learned from this was: when life gets tough, it's a sign from the universe that it's time to pack up and go home. How wrong was I?! If you've been overprotected too, you might relate. Overcoming challenges builds confidence, but you might never have had the chance to overcome any.

I didn't learn that it's OK to struggle, to stumble and even to face-plant along the path of life. And that next, you have to get up, shake it off and keep going. I now know difficulties are to be expected. That success comes to those willing to stick at it long enough for it to finally work out. And that in order to move over the bumps without breaking, you need to be as flexible as possible. I've learned there are multiple good outcomes, and it's OK not to get the one I've got fixed in my head.

I also know I need to embrace challenges rather than letting them floor me. When the unbearable feelings of resistance and wanting to give up kick in and I feel the urge to run, I take it as a sign that I'm about to go over the hump of a bump. If I can just keep going, I'll be on the downward slope.

Taking healthy risks

By challenging ourselves in small ways, we learn to deal with difficult emotions, and so feel stronger and more resilient. Maybe it's time to take a few risks? Especially as studies suggest that women are more risk-averse than men.[1] What's more, when under stress, we become even more risk-shy, while men become the opposite.[2]

Avoid risks and not only will you miss out on opportunities, but also on the chance to learn and to grow in confidence. If you're saying, 'How can I do this – I don't dare to take risks in the first place,' don't worry, you can start small.

I have found that taking on a physical challenge can have a knock-on effect on confidence in every area of your life. Recently, I went to visit a friend's new apartment in a stylish high-rise in north London. I stepped out on to the balcony to admire the view of the impressive skyline and, instantly, was hit by nausea. I quickly retreated inside, only able to check out the view from behind the sliding glass door. I'd thought I was OK with heights, but realized that over the past few years I'd become increasingly uneasy about them.

Then, a week or so later, my best friend announced the plan for her husband's birthday: a treetop zip-wiring adventure at Go Ape in a local woodland. My heart sank. Given my balcony wobble, the thought of climbing up a forty-foot tree and flinging myself off seemed an ordeal I'd rather avoid.

However, I feigned excitement, knowing I had to face my fear. As I climbed the first tree, clammy hands checking again that my harness was correctly attached, I felt my heart exploding out of my chest. I took deep breaths and told myself, 'You've got this,' a mantra I repeated all the way around the course. At Go Ape, it's your responsibility to ensure you're securely attached to the tree and the zip lines at all times, so you have to trust yourself. I finally made it up to the highest point, and zip-lined down, screaming – half exhilarated, half terrified – all the way. I can't deny I was relieved to feel the earth beneath my feet, but I also felt empowered.

Taking that risk taught me I could handle more than I'd assumed. Once you've walked a tightrope at forty feet, asking your boss if you can leave early on Friday will seem like less of a big deal. Once you've skinny-dipped with your yoga retreat sisters, confronting a friend about the money she owes you will seem easier. Surfing a five-foot wave, trekking through a jungle, running a half marathon or abseiling down a cliff face will all do the same.

I'm not suggesting you engage in truly risky behaviours; please don't start texting while driving or having unprotected sex in the name of growing your confidence. For this strategy to work, it needs to be a healthy risk and within safe parameters.

Your challenge doesn't even need to be dangerous at all, in fact. It just needs to challenge you – and for you to stick at it. 'In the past few years I have taken up hillwalking and it is helping to toughen me up,' says Karen, an artist, aged thirty-one. 'At the start of the walk I always struggle. I get a pounding headache, my hearing goes funny and I just want to turn back. But so far, I never have. I always make it to the top.'

. . . .

Exercise: make a list of healthy risks

What kinds of healthy risks or challenges could you take on to grow your confidence and courage? Brainstorm some ideas, then take some action towards actually doing one of them in the next couple of weeks.

. . . .

Summary

★ You are already strong and resilient; it's built into your DNA!

★ Bumps in the road are normal, not a sign you should give up.

★ Physical challenges and taking healthy risks can help grow your resilience and confidence.

CHAPTER 41

Name and tame your emotions

I used to find emotions very confusing. I knew I felt 'bad' but I couldn't pin down exactly what was up. I didn't have the vocabulary or understanding about all our various emotions to be able to identify what I was actually feeling. And as psychologist Susan David, author of *Emotional Agility* explains, the result of not being able to do this leaves people confused and stuck in whatever unpleasant emotion is happening. David says that 'labelling emotions is fundamental to our ability to be able to thrive'.

Neuroscience supports this approach. Studies have found that putting feelings into words helps us to manage them by calming down the stress response.[1] In short, when we name the emotion, we tame it. As a result, we feel more resourceful and we grow our resilience toolkit.

David's strategy to help you get to know your emotions is this: for each feeling you think you're experiencing, try to think of two other emotions that more accurately describe your state. For example, you may think you're 'stressed'. But this isn't an accurate enough word because 'stressed' is a blanket term we use to describe a range of emotions. Could what you're feeling, in fact, be hurt or angry or helpless? Or all three?

When I tried this out, after an argument with Aidan, at first glance I described myself as 'anxious'. But when I looked more closely, what I was actually feeling was rejected. I also noticed some sadness and under that, inadequacy. There was a real difference between what I'd first thought I was feeling and what was actually going on. And unless we know exactly what it is we're feeling, it's hard to take the right action to help ourselves.

The Feelings Wheel

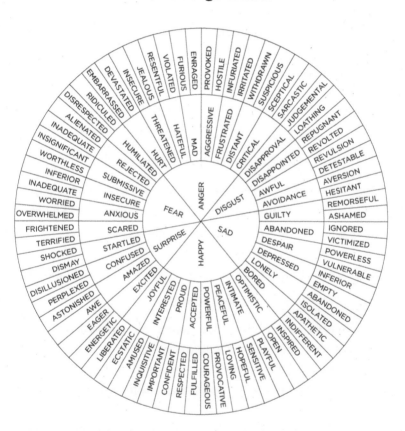

The Feelings Wheel lists the range of different emotions that we can experience. The more generic emotion words you might use are in the centre. As you work outwards, it helps you pinpoint and label exactly the emotion(s) you're feeling. Think you feel sad? Use the wheel and you may realize you actually feel isolated. Assume you're angry? Your underlying emotion may be hurt.

Another way to name and tame is to talk to someone or write about how you're feeling. Or you can try 'noticing'. This means saying to yourself, 'I'm noticing that I am feeling rejected.' It's another way to label our emotions and it also helps us step back from them. Noticing creates space between us and the emotion; we're able to observe it rather than getting pulled into it. As a result, we may be more able to take positive action to help ourselves.

. . . .

Exercise: notice how you're feeling

Find two specific words from the outer edges of the Feelings Wheel that describe what you're feeling right now. Say to yourself 'I am noticing that I am feeling . . . and . . .'

Summary

★ We often label our emotions inaccurately, meaning that we respond in the wrong way.

★ Labelling emotions helps us feel calmer and more resourceful, so try to be as specific as possible.

CHAPTER 42

Put yourself first

Women have to take the time to focus on
our mental health – take time for self, for the
spiritual, without feeling guilty or selfish. The world
will see you the way you see you, and treat you
the way you treat yourself.

BEYONCÉ, *ELLE* MAGAZINE, APRIL 2016

Imagine your best friend thinks she's just 'messed up' a job interview and so won't get the job. She comes over to your house in tears. You let her in, and before she's had a chance to speak, you say to her, 'You idiot! This is sooooo typical of you! I can't believe you've done this again! You should lie in bed awake tonight and have a long, hard think about what a loser you are!'

Now, obviously, this would never happen. We would never say this sort of thing to a friend. Because it certainly wouldn't help her (and she wouldn't be your friend for long!). So why do we think it's OK to do it to ourselves?!

What would you probably do for her? You'd likely make her a cup of tea, give her a huge hug and cook her a nourishing meal. Maybe you'd run her a bath and give her a shoulder rub too. You'd remind her how brilliant she is and tell her it will all be OK.

Treat yourself as you would a good friend

We instinctively know being kind and taking care of a friend is what will help her the most. So how come we don't do this for ourselves when we're struggling? Self-care is simply doing the things that help you to feel nurtured and loved. This will cushion you against life's knocks and bumps, and give you resources to spare.

Do you cringe at the word 'self-care' because it sounds self-indulgent? It's much more than just bubble baths and listening to pan-pipe music. Far from being selfish, self-care is an essential and useful strategy. I believe it's important to do something for self-care each day, to stay strong and anchor our resilience. It's about keeping your own tank full rather than running on empty.

What works as self-care is different for everyone. How do you find your personal strategies? Try anything which helps you to feel taken care of, loved and nurtured. A few years ago, Steph, thirty-five, had depression and anxiety that was so bad, she rarely left her flat. 'Now I manage my anxiety with regular yoga, make sure I see family and friends and am eating well, put time in to relax and to get creative by cooking and baking new recipes.'

Your strategies might be asking your partner if they can do the washing this week or saying 'no thanks' to an invitation and staying in instead. It might be breaking up with an energy-draining friend or going to bed at 8.30 p.m. tonight because that's what your body needs.

Exercise: **list your self-care essentials**

Make a list of fifteen activities which feel like self-care for you. It could be having a bath, taking the dog for a walk, calling a friend, giving yourself a facial, knitting, taking three deep breaths, getting a massage or baking a pie.

Schedule a couple into your diary for the coming week, even if it's just for ten minutes.

Exercise: **design a resilience-building experiment**

I'm always looking for little ways to challenge myself and so build my confidence and resilience. It could be sparking up a conversation with the man making my cappuccino despite the fact I don't feel like chatting, asking for feedback at every opportunity, or saying yes to something I'm nervous to do. The principle is: you try something, you survive it . . . then you're all the stronger for it.

Your experiment might be doing something imperfectly in front of others, saying no, doing something a bit 'weird' such as singing as you walk down the street, saying something you've been holding back, or sharing a struggle with a friend. Anything that's a bit out of your comfort zone will work. Challenging yourself in this way will build your resilience and give you the sense you can take on the next challenge. Remember, don't wait to feel confident before taking action . . . take action and you'll feel confident.

Summary

★ If you wouldn't say it to your best friend, don't say it to yourself.

★ Work out what feels like self-care for you and schedule it into your diary.

CHAPTER 43

Setting goals and going for your dreams

Whether you think you can, or you think you can't –
you're probably right.

HENRY FORD

At the age of thirteen, right before the era of binge drinking and boys, I was one of the sporty girls. As I was on the school teams for athletics, hockey and netball, I spent many a cold evening after school training on the floodlit AstroTurf.

I wore a stopwatch on a nylon string around my neck, and I'd jog on the spot alongside my friends who were hanging out in the park near our estate. I didn't have much money to spend on clothes, but I spent my babysitting wages on the latest Adidas gear, which I'd wear on a near-daily basis: a navy-blue shell suit with three bright orange stripes along the sides.

I remember one particular athletics event at school that felt like a very big deal. I was running the 800 metres, and my family and several friends were in attendance, carrying large banners emblazoned with the cringeworthy slogan: 'Go, Clo, Go!'

My main competition was a girl named Sam Black. Sam was known as the best runner in the school. She had a professional coach. And she was one of the popular girls. The word on the playground was, Sam couldn't be beaten.

The day is a hazy memory, but I do vividly recall the final moments of the race. I'd assumed Sam would be way ahead of me so it was a shock when I looked to the right and saw we were neck and neck. As we pulled into the last 100 metres, I saw Sam sprint past me. She won the race.

I'd been so close to winning, and yet it had never occurred to me that I could actually beat Sam. I realized I'd decided I was coming second before the race even started. I'd told myself, 'Winning's not for me.' I've often wondered, if I'd had a touch more self-belief, could I have won that day? If I'd believed I could have beaten her, would I have been the first to start sprinting at the end? I'll never know. Hindsight has made me acutely aware of one thing: unless we believe we can succeed, we're unlikely to.

Maybe you're making yourself small in some way, too? Work is a classic place to do so. In my first job after university, I worked in advertising. Unlike my colleagues, I had no intention of going for a promotion. I was the first person to volunteer to make the tea or run an errand, not believing I could do much more. It felt much safer to sit back and watch other people go for it. That's not for me, I told myself. I kept myself small.

I don't believe in telling people they can do anything they want regardless of the facts – I mean, no one's suggesting it's helpful to tell a tone-deaf teenager they have a shot at *The X Factor*, or someone who clearly isn't a natural sprinter that they could be the next Jessica Ennis-Hill. But most of us are capable of much more than we think. And when you believe in yourself, you're more likely to take action to make it a reality.

If it's been possible for someone else, it's probably possible for you

Every day, people grow their confidence; they launch businesses, they travel the world or they tell their mothers-in-law they're not coming for Christmas this year. Many of the things you want to do have been done before by other people. People thought running a mile in under four minutes was impossible before Roger Bannister did it in 1954. Soon afterwards, many others managed it too. If someone else has done what you want to do, chances are it's at least possible for you, too. There is nothing so special about you – and I mean that in the best way. Your brain is plastic; at a physical level, it changes and adapts all the time, allowing you to learn and change.

Who else do you know who's done what you want to do? Can you learn from or gain inspiration from them? Read books, listen to podcasts, attend talks and meet people for coffee to immerse yourself in the mindsets of people who have done what you want to do.

Giving yourself permission

It sounds odd that we should need 'permission' to go after what we want, but I hear women say this is true for them, time and again. I know that if you've been raised to be a 'good girl' you'll relate to this. We ask ourselves, 'Who am I to be a leader?', 'Who am I to put my work out there?' or 'What will people think?' We question if we're allowed to even ask for what we want.

It's as if we're waiting for someone to validate us and tell us it's OK before we trust ourselves. Having someone truly believe in you – your partner, a mentor or your boss – is incredible, but the person who needs to give you permission, is you. So give yourself permission to dream. Give yourself permission to think about what you really want and to pursue it bravely. Give yourself permission to be confident, to fake it until you make it. And most importantly, give yourself permission to risk failing because it will absolutely be worth it.

Get your subconscious mind on board

In 2017, I made a lot of my goals a reality. My first book *The Anxiety Solution* was a bestseller on Amazon, it was featured in the *Daily Mail* several times and I was invited to speak at events I'd always wanted to speak at. As well as all that, I was able to take a month off to travel. Yes, there was an element of luck and hard work involved but these were the exact things I'd written down in my journal, almost every day of 2016. I'm convinced writing down my goals helped make them a reality.

Some people would call this 'manifesting', a mystical force of attraction that says focusing on what you want will magnetically draw it towards you. But I'd be more likely to explain it this way: what looks like magic happens because when you put your attention on what you want, it helps you spot opportunities to make it happen.

The key to this is writing and accountability. The act of writing down goals and intentions helps us to encode them more deeply into our minds. The science backs this up; a study at Dominican University in California found that we're 32 per cent more likely to achieve our goals if we write them down and tell a friend about them.[1] Writing puts your subconscious on alert for ways to take action towards what you're aiming for. Telling a friend helps to make it more 'real' – plus they can hold you to account. These strategies are the opposite of out of sight, out of mind – you are keeping your goals front and centre at all times.

A fun way to do this is to get yourself into the mindset of having already achieved the goal. Then you write about it as a done deal, with you already proud, excited, celebrating or grateful to have achieved it. The idea is, associating the goal with a positive feeling helps you to cement it in your mind even more powerfully.

Examples might be:

- 'I'm so proud I'm now confident to speak in public.'
- 'I am loving having completed my diploma in counselling.'
- 'I'm celebrating having saved £5,000 for a dream trip.'
- 'I'm excited to have been promoted to sales manager.'
- 'I am enjoying being anxiety-free for the past six months.'

. . . .

Exercise: make your goals real

Make a daily – or weekly, if daily seems unmanageable – list of your goals. Write them as if they've already happened, including the positive feeling they will bring.

. . . .

Don't go to sleep without doing this

Your brain is a creative, problem-solving machine. Have you ever noticed how you go to sleep on an issue and wake up with renewed clarity, a perfect solution, or a new creative idea? Studies have found the REM stage of sleep, when you dream, is involved in creative problem-solving.[2] As you sleep, the subconscious ticks away, accessing your memories, wisdom and experience to find an answer.

So tonight, don't go to sleep without asking your subconscious mind to work on a problem for you. Setting an intention before you go to sleep is a powerful tool in the realization of your goals. Here's how I harness my brain's ability: as if I'm talking to Siri, I literally say out loud, 'Subconscious, I'd like to work on you helping me to wake up more calm and confident tomorrow / give me creative ideas for this chapter I'm writing / find solutions for what I can do to help this client.' It sounds a bit far out, but it works.

. . . .

Exercise: harness the power of sleep

Plan this evening's problem solving by finishing the following sentence. 'Tonight I'm going to ask my subconscious for help with . . .'

. . . .

Your self-talk

Whenever you're doing something new, reaching outside your comfort zone or going after something which means a lot to you, it will undoubtedly trigger negative self-talk. Rest assured you're not alone. This is just a protective part of you, trying to keep you safe from the possibility, you know, of making a fool of yourself and dying because you got kicked out of the tribe.

You know this extreme fear is an evolutionary leftover so isn't rational or helpful now. But I promise you, even super-confident people will still have an aspect of negative inner chatter; *the difference is whether you listen to it or not.* Remember the steps from Chapter 5 'Reboot your beliefs' – be aware of this negative voice. Thank it for trying to help you. Think of what a friend would say instead. And choose to take action anyway.

Questioning your thoughts is also key; don't let thoughts run riot. Ask yourself: 'Is that really true?' 'Can I absolutely know that it's true?'

Here are some examples:

- 'I'll make a fool of myself.' → Is that really true? Can you absolutely know that that's true?
- 'My family will think I'm getting too big for my boots.' → Is that really true? Am I a mind-reader?
- 'I've always lacked confidence and I'll never change.' → Is that really true? Never? Do I have a crystal ball that can predict the future?

. . . .

Exercise: check your self-talk

Notice what you're saying to yourself. Set a calendar alert to check in with yourself during the day and notice how you're speaking to yourself. Is it kind? Is it constructive? Would you speak to your best friend that way? If not, it needs to change.

. . . .

Celebrate the goals you do reach

'I'm hard on myself when I don't meet my goals, or if things don't go 100 per cent to plan,' Jenna, twenty-eight, who works in marketing, told me. 'I have found that even the goals I reach,

I don't celebrate reaching. It's like I'm always looking for the next thing.'

So many people are like Jenna. They achieve a goal and simply move on to the next milestone. But it's time for you to begin celebrating and acknowledging your every success. Otherwise, you'll feel as if you're on an endless treadmill with no opportunity to bask in your awesomeness. Even if you only get part of the way to your goal, celebrate that too. It's progress – and that is a wonderful thing.

Be kind, whether you reach the stars or not

We've all heard the saying, 'Reach for the stars, and at least if you fail, you'll reach the moon.' Unless we stretch ourselves, we won't get anywhere near close to where we want to be. But nobody is perfect, and you might not reach every goal you set yourself. Be a kind, loving friend to yourself no matter what; giving it a try is brave, and doing your best is all that is required.

Step back and enjoy the view

It's easy to discount the progress you've already made, the challenges you've overcome and the things you've learned. You're always up close and personal with yourself, so it can be hard to appreciate the bigger picture of who you are and what you've achieved. Take some time to step back from yourself and admire the view. Exercises like the career timeline in Chapter 7 'Meet your inner imposter' will help you to remember the unique qualities and skills that helped get you where you already are.

Look below the surface

When I was training as a professional business and life coach, one of the key things we learned was always to consider the whole iceberg. When it comes to setting goals, we're often only aware of the top section of the iceberg; the things we can see and are consciously aware of. But underneath the waterline, there is a huge mass of beliefs, conditioning and past experiences that can hold us back.

'My dream is to be a yoga teacher,' Natalie, thirty, who's currently a retail assistant, told me. 'I wanted to sign up for training for ages, but I kept putting it off.'

When Natalie was brave enough to peek beneath the surface, she discovered what was holding her back. She told me, 'I keep telling myself I'm not good enough. I think my family, friends and workmates will laugh or say I can't do it.'

We have already looked at beliefs quite a bit in the course of this book, in Parts One and Two. Once Natalie challenged her unhelpful beliefs, she was able to sign up for her dream. These questions can help reveal your unhelpful beliefs and help you to challenge them, too. Ask yourself:

- 'What is stopping me?'
- 'What's really stopping me?'
- 'If I knew I couldn't fail, what would I do?'
- 'What would I need to believe, in order to move forward?'

· ·

Exercise: **talk back to your limiting beliefs**

Identify your limiting beliefs. Then answer back to each belief as though it's coming from a wise, rational and loving friend. For example:

'I'll never be good enough to succeed.' → You cannot predict the future. You have been good enough for many things in life, such as holding down a great job and having a great relationship. This might be challenging, but you're more than capable.

'I am broken and can't be fixed.' → There is nothing so special about you that you can't feel better. No one is inherently broken. Progress can always happen and change is inevitable. Look at how far you've already come!

'I'm not smart enough.' → Smart enough for what? To take a tiny step forward? You have been smart enough for a lot of things, like managing projects at work and getting a good degree.

Summary

★ Believing you can do something is an important part of helping you to reach your goals.

★ Writing down your goals and intentions helps you to make them a reality.

★ Be mindful of your self-talk when you're going out of your comfort zone, and always be kind to yourself.

CHAPTER 44

Stop thinking, start doing

If you hear a voice within you say, 'You cannot paint,'
then by all means paint, and that voice
will be silenced.
VINCENT VAN GOGH

The fastest way to cure your overthinking is to take action. What is the smallest step you can take towards your goal? Proving to yourself you can do it is the most potent way to transform your disbelief into self-belief.

You can have what you want; you just have to decide

Marie Forleo is the queen of the online coaching world. She asserts what many people have found: it's much easier to get what you want *when you know what you want*. Of the numerous clients I see in my therapy practice each week, one thing always strikes me: people are excellent at identifying what they do not want. They don't want to be anxious any more, they don't want to clam up in social situations, they don't want to stay stuck in a life that feels miserable and wrong. When I ask them what they do want, they're sometimes lost for words, often pretty vague.

Thinking about what we *do* want isn't always simple. Often, we just haven't sat down to think about it for long enough, or we haven't had the right guidance and structure to nail it down. Most likely, we haven't had the encouragement and permission we crave to dream a bit bigger. But unless you know where you're going, how are you going to get there?

Define your own version of success

What would your ideal average day be? Running your own company with a schedule full of exciting meetings? Spending time with your child and your dog in the park? Writing alone, with a view of the sea from your window? A perfect average day is different for everyone. Don't let an external idea of success dictate what your goals should be. It's OK to want what you want. You might have modest goals or wild ones; it's all good. You might have one version of your ideal day, or multiple. Explore all the possibilities without your critical mind butting in.

. . . .

Exercise: picture a perfect day

Write a few sentences about what your ideal average day(s) would be like. Keep it in the front of your mind by sticking it on the fridge, or regularly looking back in your notebook. Ask yourself: what is the one thing I can do to start to make it a reality? This example might help you start thinking.

> I get up early to do some stretches and spend 10 minutes meditating. I make a coffee and walk the dog while listening to a podcast. Next, I make pancakes for breakfast with my partner before cycling to work for 9.30 a.m. I have a focused and productive morning

working as a creative director in a fast-paced and vibrant office, before meeting a friend for lunch. After work, I go to choir or I play netball before heading home for dinner.

. . . .

Exercise: **Do, Be, Have**

I first heard of Do, Be, Have goals from the coach Denise Duffield Thomas. It's a structure for thinking about what you want, then creating goals and intentions. Don't worry about how you'll get to your goals, just allow yourself to think creatively and freely about what it is you want.

In your notebook, split the page into three and write down the following headings: Do, Be, Have. Then fill in your goals. An example might look like this:

Do	Be	Have
Climb up Mount Snowdon	Raise my level of confidence at work to an 8/10	Flexible working times at my office job
Get a promotion at work	Be confident enough in my own skin to wear a bikini on holiday	£10,000 saved in the bank for a house deposit
Train as a Pilates teacher	Be confident enough to start looking for a new job	One new client each month

Make yourself accountable

It's a dark, rainy evening and you've promised yourself you'll go to the gym. You're much more likely to make it there if you've arranged to meet a friend than if you try to go it alone (something you may have discovered in the past). Having someone to hold us accountable is a powerful factor in helping us to stick to our goals.

If you want to attend a creative writing class, simply announce it to your WhatsApp group and the positive peer pressure will encourage you to go. I have two friends who are also coaches, and when we need a boost to act out of our comfort zone, we post it in our WhatsApp group and always get a flurry of supportive messages and encouraging emojis back.

There are two kinds of accountability: negative and positive. Maybe the stick works best for you? That's you if, for example, knowing your boss would be disappointed in you for dropping out of a presentation keeps you doing it. Or perhaps you're more of a carrot person. That is, you'd get inspiration from your Facebook group cheering you on to publish your first blog post. Either way, find people to hold you accountable. There are so many options, from online groups to Meet-ups, there's no excuse to go it alone.

Here are some accountability ideas:

- Hiring a professional coach
- Getting a mentor
- Enlisting a friend (ideally one in the same boat so you can help each other)
- Creating an accountability WhatsApp group
- Joining a Facebook group

- In-person support groups
- A women's circle

Now ask yourself, who could hold you accountable?

Make your goals specific and measurable

Goals such as 'be happy' or 'become more confident' are things I hear a lot when talking to clients. Unfortunately, happiness and confidence are pretty nebulous, hard to pin down or define. Both of them go up and down on a moment-by-moment basis. And it's not easy to know when you've achieved them.

- If your goal is to earn more money, how much?
- If you want to gain more customers for your business, how many?
- If you want to make more friends, how many and what are they like?
- If you want to say 'no more', in what situations and to whom?
- If you'd like to stop people pleasing, which specific habits will you get rid of?

It makes sense to set concrete and measurable goals. What, exactly, will help you to get to a place of having more confidence? Will you meet at least one new person a week? Write down a daily list of things you've done well that day. Practise visualizing how you want a challenging conversation to go. These are called 'process goals' and they will help you to get to your end goal.

You can still measure whether your happiness or confidence, for example, are increasing, which will tell you if your process goals are helping you or if you need to change your approach. Simply rate it on a scale of 1 to 10 each week (one being the least confident and 10 being the most).

Break it down

Breaking goals down makes them seem much more manageable, FACT. What is the smallest step you can take? Then, what is the next, small step? One way to break goals down can be to put a time limit on each step. 'Doing research' can seem overwhelming and unmanageable, but what about a mini goal of just thirty minutes of research? This is much easier to achieve and will get the ball rolling while growing your momentum and your confidence. Tasks such as 'build a website' are huge and daunting – enough to make anyone want to postpone it. So what is the first teeny, tiny step you can take? For example:

Writing a novel → Research books on how to write a novel and order one from Amazon.

Starting a blog → Brainstorm ten blog titles and ask five friends for feedback.

Making two new friends → Spend thirty minutes researching and reading an article on making new friends.

Doing a presentation in front of the whole of your team → Put your hand up to ask a question at the next team meeting.

Buying a house → Download a budget template and spend twenty minutes filling it in.

Taking your anxiety from an 8/10 to a 5/10 → Spend half an hour thinking about what's worked for you in the past.

Going backpacking around Asia → Browse Lonely Planet forums for thirty minutes to get an idea of travel budgets.

Next decide when, exactly, you will do each action. I often have my clients schedule them into their diaries. If it's in the diary, its official, right? For example, put in your diary at 11 a.m. on Monday morning: *Do 30 minutes of research.*

Other questions to ask yourself:

- Who could I talk to who's done what I want to do or similar?
- Who could help me?
- Who could hold me accountable?

Final thought

If your goal isn't a bit scary, you're not aiming high enough!

Summary

★ Deciding what you actually want is an important first step to getting it.
★ Having people to hold you accountable to a goal increases your chances of reaching it.
★ Break goals into manageable chunks, making them specific and measurable.

Resources

David Allen, *Getting Things Done: The Art of Stress-free Productivity*, Piatkus, 2015

James Altucher, *The Power of No: Because One Little Word Can Bring Health, Abundance and Happiness*, Hay House, 2014

Mary Beard, *Women & Power: A Manifesto*, Profile Books, 2017

Gabrielle Bernstein, *Judgement Detox: Release the Beliefs That Hold You Back from Living a Better Life*, Hay House, 2018

Beyoncé, 'EXCLUSIVE: Beyoncé wants to change the conversation', *Elle* magazine, April 2016

Brené Brown, *Dare to Lead: Brave Work. Tough Conversations. Whole Hearts*, Vermillion, 2018

Brené Brown, *Daring Greatly: How the Courage to Be Vulnerable Transforms the Way We Live, Love, Parent and Lead*, Penguin Audiobook, 2018

Susan Cain, *Quiet: The Power of Introverts in a World That Can't Stop Talking*, Penguin, 2012

Dr Henry Cloud and Dr John Townsend, *Boundaries: When to Say Yes, How to Say No, To Take Control of Your Life*, Zondervan, 2017

Stephen Covey, *The 7 Habits of Highly Effective People: Powerful Lessons in Personal Change*, Simon & Schuster, 1989 (revised 2004)

Susan David, *Emotional Agility: Get Unstuck, Embrace Change and Thrive in Work and Life*, Penguin Life, 2017

Michelle Elman, @scarrednotscared on Instagram, and the body positive campaign 'Scarred Not Scared'

Phanella Fine and Alice Olins, *Step Up: Confidence, Success and Your Stellar Career in 10 Minutes a Day*, Ebury, 2016

Debbie Ford, *Courage: Overcoming Fear and Igniting Self-Confidence*, HarperAudio, 2013

Johann Hari, *Lost Connections: Why You're Depressed and How to Find Hope*, Bloomsbury Circus, 2018

Hilary Jacobs Hendel, *It's Not Always Depression: A New Theory of Listening to Your Body, Discovering Core Emotions and Reconnecting with Your Authentic Self*, Penguin Life, 2018

Ellen Hendriksen, *How to Be Yourself: Quiet Your Inner Critic and Rise Above Social Anxiety*, St Martin's Press, 2018

Byron Katie, *Your Inner Awakening: The Work of Byron Katie: Four Questions That Will Transform Your Life*, audio CD, read by the author, Simon & Schuster, 2007

Jessica Lahey, *The Gift of Failure: How the Best Parents Learn to Let Go So Their Children Can Succeed*, HarperCollins, 2015

Helen Lewis, *Difficult Women: A History of Feminism in 9 Fights*, Jonathan Cape, 2020

Tara Mohr, *Playing Big: A Practical Guide for Brilliant Women Like You*, Hutchinson, 2014

Caroline Paul, *The Gutsy Girl: Escapades for Your Life of Epic Adventure*, Bloomsbury, 2016

Anthony Robbins, *Awaken the Giant Within: Take Immediate Control of Your Mental, Emotional, Physical and Financial Destiny*, Simon & Schuster, 1992

Anthony Robbins, *Unlimited Power: The New Science of Personal Achievement*, Simon & Schuster, 1989

Marshall Rosenberg, *Non-Violent Communication: A Language of Life*, Puddle Dancer Press, 2003

Sheryl Sandberg, with Nell Scovell, *Lean In: Women, Work, and the Will to Lead*, W. H. Allen, 2013

Colin Tipping, *Radical Self-Forgiveness: The Direct Path to True Self-Acceptance*, Sounds True, Inc., 2010

Ekhart Tolle, *The Power of Now: A Guide to Spiritual Enlightenment*, Yellow Kite, 2001

Vanessa Van Edwards, *Captivate: The Science of Succeeding with People*, Portfolio Penguin, 2017

Bronnie Ware, *The Top Five Regrets of the Dying*, Hay House, 2012

Geoff Watts and Kim Morgan, *The Coach's Casebook: Mastering the Twelve Traits That Trap Us*, Inspect & Adapt Ltd, 2015

Sir John Whitmore, *Coaching for Performance: The Principles and Practice of Coaching and Leadership*, Nicholas Brealey, 2010

References

PART ONE
How to start the change

Chapter 1: Why I wrote this book for women

1. https://www.girlguiding.org.uk/what-we-do/our-stories-and-news/news/girls-as-young-as-seven-feel-pressure-to-look-perfect/
2. https://www.mentalhealth.org.uk/statistics/mental-health-statistics-men-and-women
3. https://www.ons.gov.uk/employmentandlabourmarket/peopleinwork/earningsandworkinghours/articles/womenshouldertheresponsibilityofunpaidwork/2016-11-10
4. https://www.ucl.ac.uk/news/2009/apr/women-tend-towards-modesty-self-estimates-intelligence
5. https://hbr.org/2014/08/why-women-dont-apply-for-jobs-unless-theyre-100-qualified
6. http://www.apa.org/pubs/journals/releases/psp-pspp0000078.pdf
7. https://www.huffingtonpost.co.uk/entry/more-than-half-of-girls-have-low-body-esteem-and-its-holding-them-back-from-key-opportunities_uk_59d399eae4b048a4432545 64
8. https://www.ncbi.nlm.nih.gov/pubmed/20919592
9. https://www.phillyvoice.com/body-image-fat-earnings-potential-career/

10. https://onlinelibrary.wiley.com/doi/abs/10.1002/eat.20483

11. https://www.ncbi.nlm.nih.gov/pmc/articles/PMC2864925/

12. https://www.ons.gov.uk/peoplepopulationandcommunity/crimeandjustice/articles/abuseduringchildhood/findingsfromtheyearendingmarch2016crimesurveyforenglandandwales

13. https://www.ons.gov.uk/peoplepopulationandcommunity/crimeandjustice/articles/sexualoffencesinenglandandwales/yearendingmarch2017

14. https://www.ons.gov.uk/peoplepopulationandcommunity/crimeandjustice/bulletins/crimeinenglandandwales/yearendingseptember2017

Chapter 3: Believe you can change

1. https://www.theatlantic.com/education/archive/2016/12/how-praise-became-a-consolation-prize/510845/

PART TWO
How to learn to listen to your own voice

Chapter 4: Freeing yourself from what other people think

1. http://journals.sagepub.com/doi/10.1177/1948550617732388

Chapter 7: **Meet your inner imposter**

1. http://www.rookiemag.com/2013/05/emma-watson-interview/
2. https://twitter.com/mindykaling/status/475515607698243584

Chapter 8: **Learn to love compliments**

1. https://www.sciencedirect.com/science/article/pii/S0022103116302943
2. http://journals.plos.org/plosone/article?id=10.1371/journal.pone.0048174

PART THREE
How to stop apologizing for yourself – and say NO

Chapter 10: **Shatter the illusion of perfectionism**

1. https://www.mckendree.edu/academics/scholars/issue18/gawlik.htm
2. https://www.theguardian.com/lifeandstyle/2016/oct/04/girls-as-young-as-7-feel-pressure-to-be-pretty-body-confidence-girlguiding-study-reveals

Chapter 12: **The strength of setting boundaries**

1. https://www.psychologytoday.com/us/blog/traversing-the-inner-terrain/201705/the-right-boundary

Chapter 14: **Discover the power of 'no'**

1. https://www.youtube.com/watch?v=DyM7vi1HMvM
2. https://www.theguardian.com/lifeandstyle/womens-blog/2015/aug/20/why-should-women-run-the-gauntlet-of-harassment-while-out-jogging

PART FOUR
How to fail yourself better

Chapter 16: **Freeing yourself from fear of failure**

1. https://www.forbes.com/sites/womensmedia/2018/06/14/why-some-women-fear-taking-risks-and-what-were-not-doing-about-it/#214459fc67da

PART FIVE
How to heal shame and self-doubt

Chapter 20: **Bringing shame into the light**

1. http://www.pnas.org/content/113/10/2625

Chapter 23: **Owning your body**

1. https://www.huffingtonpost.com/entry/time-to-defund-the-diet-industry_us_58c2b63ee4b0c3276fb783c7
2. https://www.researchandmarkets.com/reports/3133911/global-cosmetic-surgery-and-service-market-report

PART SIX

How to stand up and be heard

Chapter 24: **How to find your voice**

1. http://time.com/3666135/sheryl-sandberg-talking-while-female-manterruptions/

Chapter 26: **Find the courage to be criticized**

1. https://hbr.org/2013/07/connect-then-lead

Chapter 27: **Why role models matter**

1. https://www.ncbi.nlm.nih.gov/pubmed/1301372

Chapter 28: **How to speak in public**

1. https://www.hbs.edu/faculty/Pages/item.aspx?num=45869

Chapter 29: **Learn the art of communication**

1. http://journals.sagepub.com/doi/abs/10.1177/0261927X14533197?papetoc=& Manterruption is real
2. https://slate.com/human-interest/2014/07/study-men-interrupt-women-more-in-tech-workplaces-but-high-ranking-women-learn-to-interrupt.html
3. https://www.washingtonpost.com/news/powerpost/wp/2016/09/13/white-house-women-are-now-in-the-room-where-it-happens/?noredirect=on&utm_term=.d257380437b8

4. https://link.springer.com/article/10.1007/BF00986997#page-1
5. https://journals.plos.org/plosone/article?id=10.1371/journal.pone.0097506
6. http://www.allisonshapira.com/how-can-you-speak-with-power-and-avoid-vocal-fry/

Chapter 31: Asking for what you want at work

1. https://www.bbc.co.uk/news/business-43632763
2. https://hbr.org/2018/06/research-women-ask-for-raises-as-often-as-men-but-are-less-likely-to-get-them
3. https://timewise.co.uk/wp-content/uploads/2018/05/Manifesto-for-change.pdf
4. http://www.smeweb.com/2017/11/09/nine-ten-say-flexible-working-boosts-productivity/
5. https://www.gov.uk/flexible-working
6. http://timewise.co.uk/wp-content/uploads/2014/06/Updated-A-flexible-future-for-Britain.pdf

Chapter 35: How to grow your social confidence

1. https://guilfordjournals.com/doi/abs/10.1521/jscp.23.6.792.54800

References

PART SEVEN
How to find the real you and what she wants to do

Chapter 39: **Be the real you**

1. https://www.ons.gov.uk/peoplepopulationandcommunity/
    wellbeing/articles/lonelinesswhatcharacteristicsand
    circumstancesareassociatedwithfeelinglonely/2018-04-10

Chapter 40: **Stronger, wiser, smarter: how to be resilient**

1. https://www.sciencedirect.com/science/article/pii/
    S0167268111001521
2. https://journals.sagepub.com/doi/
    abs/10.1177/0963721411429452

Chapter 41: **Name and tame your emotions**

1. https://www.ncbi.nlm.nih.gov/pubmed/17576282

Chapter 43: **Setting goals and going for your dreams**

1. https://www.dominican.edu/dominicannews/study-
    highlights-strategies-for-achieving-goals
2. https://www.ncbi.nlm.nih.gov/pmc/articles/
    PMC2700890/

Index